LINDA LAWRE

CHE
26 ROUNDH,
LEEDS LS7 1 AB
Tel: 0532 425996

10 Minute Guide to Windows™ 3.1

Kate Barnes

A Division of Prentice Hall Computer Publishing
201 W. 103rd Street, Indianapolis, IN 46290 USA

International Standard Book Number: 0-672-30052-4

96 95   15 14 13

Interpretation of the printing code: the rightmost double-digit number is the year of the book's first printing; the rightmost single-digit number is the number of the book's printing. For example, a printing code of 92-1 shows that this copy of the book was printed during the first printing of the book in 1992.

Publisher: *Richard K. Swadley*
Associate Publisher: *Marie Butler-Knight*
Managing Editor: *Elizabeth Keaffaber*
Senior Development Editor: *Lisa Bucki*
Development Editors: *Gregg Bushyeager, Faithe Wempen*
Copy Editors: *Howard Peirce, Ronda Henry*
Cover Design: *Dan Armstrong*
Indexer: *John Sleeva*
Production Team: *Brad Chinn, Brook Farling, Joelynn Gifford, Denny Hager, Debbie Hanna, Michelle Laseau, Bob LaRoche, David McKenna, Matthew Morrill, Juli Pavey, Joe Ramon, Caroline Roop, Mary Beth Wakefield, Corinne Walls, Jenny Watson*

Special thanks to Hilary Adams for assuring the technical accuracy of this book.

Screen reproductions in this book were created by means of the program Collage Plus from Inner Media, Inc., Hollis, NH.

Printed in the United States of America

Contents

Introduction

"There aren't enough hours in the day." It's a common complaint. Time is a commodity everyone can use more of. When it comes to working with your computer, Windows can save you time. How? Windows makes the computer easier to use and increases the "fun factor."

The What and Why of Windows

Windows is a Graphical User Interface (GUI). This GUI comes with useful applications, including a word processor (Write), a graphics program (Paintbrush), and a communications program (Terminal). It also contains some nifty accessories that no work area should be without, such as a calendar, calculator, and notepad.

> **Graphical User Interface** A GUI (pro-
> nounced "gooey") is a way to interact with your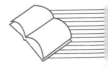
> computer. You usually use a mouse to point at
> and select icons (small pictures that most often
> represent files or application programs) as well
> as choose operations (commands from menus)
> on those icons. A GUI is an alternative to a
> *command-line interface*, where text commands
> are entered from the keyboard.

Why use Windows? Windows makes using your computer faster and easier in the following ways:

- You can work on more than one file at a time within a single application program. This allows you to copy information from one file to the other, without wasting time retyping information.

- You can also work in more than one application at a time. By choosing a simple menu command, you can switch between applications without having to close one to open the other. You can also copy information from one application to the other.

- Windows' graphical user interface is easy to figure out and remember, so you'll be up and running quickly. Once you get started, you'll be surprised how quickly your "educated guesses" become correct ones.

- All application programs designed for Windows use similar keyboard and mouse operations to select objects and choose commands. To a great extent, when you've learned one application, you've learned part of them all.

Windows' GUI provides a common approach to using a variety of applications for your computer. With just a little effort, Windows is fast, easy, and fun to learn.

Why the 10 Minute Guide to Windows 3.1?

The *10 Minute Guide to Windows 3.1* can save even more of your precious time. Each lesson is designed to be completed in 10 minutes or less, so you'll be up to snuff in basic Windows skills in around four hours.

Though you can jump between lessons, starting at the beginning is a good plan. The bare-bones basics are covered first; more advanced topics are covered later. Whatever you do, don't miss the inside front and back covers. The inside front cover of this book features instructions for installing Windows on your system.

Conventions Used in this Book

To help you move through the lessons easily, these conventions are used:

On-screen text	On-screen text will appear in a special computer font.
What you type	Information you type will appear in a bold, color, computer font.
Items you select	Commands, options, and icons you select or keys you press will appear in color.
Selection keys	Boldface letters within a menu title, menu option, or dialog option indicate selection keys for keyboard shortcuts. These correspond to the underlined letters on-screen.

In addition to these conventions, the *10 Minute Guide to Windows 3.1* uses the following icons to identify helpful information:

Plain English   New or unfamiliar terms are defined in (you got it) "plain English."

 Timesaver Tips   Look here for ideas that cut corners and confusion.

 Panic Button   This icon identifies areas where new users often run into trouble and offers practical solutions.

For More Information . . .

Once you've learned all this book has to offer, you'll be a fairly confident user. You'll also find it a useful resource to brush up on procedures. If you want to learn more about Windows, Que offers these titles:

The First Book of Windows 3.1, Second Edition, by Jack Nimersheim.

Windows 3.1 Bible, by Hoffman and Sosinsky.

1-800-HELP with Windows, by Carl Townsend.

Trademarks

All terms mentioned in this book that are known to be trademarks or service marks are listed below. In addition, terms suspected of being trademarks or service marks have been appropriately capitalized. Sams cannot attest to the accuracy of this information. Use of a term in this book should not be regarded as affecting the validity of any trademark or service mark.

Microsoft Windows, Microsoft Write, Microsoft Paintbrush, and Microsoft Word are registered trademarks of Microsoft Corporation.

WordPerfect for Windows is a registered trademark of WordPerfect Corporation.

Lessons

Lesson 1
Starting
Windows

In this lesson, you will learn how to start Windows and to recognize what you see when you get there.

Starting Windows

To start Windows, follow these steps:

1. Begin at the C prompt (or the prompt for the drive where Windows is installed). If you are not at the correct prompt, type the drive designation (such as `c:`) and press **Enter**.

2. Once you are at the correct prompt, type `win` and press **Enter**.

If Nothing Happens   If you type `win` and get a message like `Bad command or file name`, Windows is probably not installed on your computer. Refer to the inside front cover of this book for installation instructions or consult the *Windows User's Guide* to install Windows.

Once you have successfully started Windows, the Windows Title screen (including the version number) briefly appears. Next, the opening screen appears (see Figure 1.1).

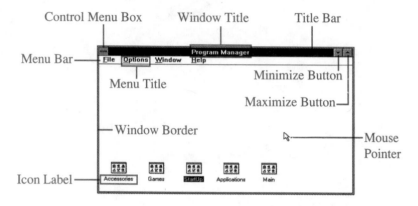

Figure 1.1 The opening screen showing the Program Manager window.

The Opening Screen

As you can see in Figure 1.1, the opening screen is made up of several components. These components are used throughout Windows and Windows applications to make it easy for you to get your work done.

The components of a window include:

Border Identifies the edge of the window.

Window Title Identifies the window and (often) suggests the use of the window.

Title Bar   Gives added information, such as a document name if you are working with a document in the window.

Desktop   This is the area outside the windows.

Mouse Pointer   The pointer (usually an arrow) on-screen that allows you to select items and choose commands. Move the mouse pointer and select items by clicking the mouse button. See Lesson 2 for more information about using the mouse.

Minimize and Maximize Buttons   Click on these buttons to make the active window smaller or larger. Once the window is full-screen size, a button called the *Restore button* allows you to restore the window to its previous (smaller) size.

Icon   The Program Manager uses two types of icons. The first type is called a *group icon* (see Figure 1.1). Group icons allow you to organize your software programs in much the same way you would organize a filing cabinet. (Word processor and spreadsheet go in the Applications group, Calculator and Notepad go in the Accessories group, etc.) The second type, *program-item icons,* are displayed in a window when you open a group icon. Program-item icons represent programs (Microsoft Excel, WordPerfect, and so on) that you have on your computer. There are many other types of icons used throughout Windows and Windows applications. They will be pointed out as they are introduced in the book.

Control Menu Box   Used to access the Control menu, from which you may change the size of the window, close a window, or switch to another window.

3

Menu Bar   Displays the menu titles you select to access the commands contained in the menu. Each application might have different menu titles, but you access the menus in the same fashion. For more on menus, see Lesson 4. Figure 1.2 shows the menu commands available in the File menu.

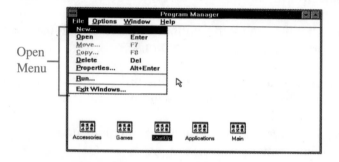

Figure 1.2   The Program Manager File menu.

How Windows is Organized

It is no accident that the Program Manager appears when you start Windows. The Program Manager is the heart of Windows. From here you may access any of the applications that came with Windows or any applications you have installed.

What Is a Program Manager Group?   A Program Manager *group* is nothing more than a window containing a collection of related program-item icons.

When you first install Windows, several groups are created automatically. The Main group contains the following Windows applications:

Control Panel   The Control Panel contains the controls for the Windows environment. From the Control Panel, you can change the colors of screen, control the sensitivity of the mouse and keyboard, and access many other features of Windows.

File Manager   Helps you manage the files and directories on your disk. You can use File Manager to move or copy files to a different directory or disk, delete files, open applications and print files.

Print Manager   Acts as the "middleman" between your application and the printer. When you print a file in Windows, it is sent to the Print Manager which in turn sends it to the printer.

Windows Setup   Allows you to add components to Windows that were not included when Windows was installed. Setup also allows you to add applications to run in Windows.

Tutorial   Offers a "guided tour" of Windows. This icon will be present if you choose to include the Tutorial in the installation process.

PIF Editor   PIF files contain information used by Windows to run non-Windows applications. This includes file names, memory requirements, etc. Windows 3.1 provides PIF files for more non-Windows applications than ever before and the PIF Editor allows you to configure them.

Clipboard Viewer Allows you to view and save Clipboard images. The Clipboard serves as a temporary storage area when you copy something from one application to be pasted into another.

DOS Shell For you diehard DOS prompt (C:>) lovers, the DOS Shell lets you jump out of Windows to the DOS prompt without actually exiting Windows.

Other groups include Accessories (containing Write, Paintbrush, and other helpful tools), Games, StartUp, and Applications.

Leaving So Soon? Just in case you want to take a break before starting Lesson 2, here is how you can exit Windows. From the Program Manager window (see Figure 1.1), press and hold down the Alt key, and press F4. Windows will ask you to confirm that you want to exit the program. Press Enter to confirm and exit or Esc to cancel and remain in Windows.

In this lesson, you learned how to start Windows, and you learned the major components of the opening screen. In the next lesson, you'll learn how to use the mouse.

Lesson 2

Navigating the Desktop with the Mouse

In this lesson, you will learn how to use the mouse to make selections and change the appearance of the screen.

Mouse Basics

The mouse is often favored over the keyboard by both novice and experienced computer users. You can use the mouse to select objects, change the appearance of the screen and choose commands for Windows to perform. You don't *have* to use a mouse. All mouse operations have keyboard equivalents. Instructions for using both the keyboard and mouse are included in this book.

You'll see certain terms used throughout this chapter as well as the remainder of the book (such as *point, drag,* and *click*). Now is the time to become thoroughly familiar with these terms.

Selecting or Choosing Objects

You can use the mouse to quickly select an icon, window, or menu command. This is a two-step process:

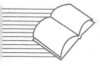

Point To point at an object (icon, menu title or command, window title bar, and so on), move the mouse across your desk or mouse pad so the mouse cursor (usually a pointer) touches the object. You may have to pick up the mouse and reposition it if you run out of room on your desk.

Simply pointing at an object doesn't give Windows enough information to do anything. To select an object or choose a command, click the left mouse button on the object you are pointing at.

Click to Select After pointing at an object (menu title, icon, and so on) you can click on it to select it. Quickly press and release the left mouse button once. If the object is an icon or window, it will become highlighted. If you click on a menu title, the menu will open.

Try clicking the mouse. Click once on the **Control Menu** box in the upper left corner of the Program Manager window. You'll see menu options for sizing the Program Manager window, closing the Program Manager, and switching applications. You can make the menu disappear by clicking outside the menu. If you prefer to use the keyboard, press **Esc** to close the menu.

Opening or Closing a Window

Double-clicking an object is a shortcut to open a group window or program-item from an icon. Double-clicking on the window control box is a shortcut to closing a window.

Double-Click to Open or Close Some operations require that you *double-click* on an object. As the name suggests, a double-click is simply two clicks of the left mouse button in rapid succession.

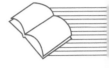

For example, point at the Accessories icon and double-click. If you do it correctly, the Accessories icon opens up to the Accessories window. You can double-click to open an icon to its window. You can also double-click on a window's Control Menu box. This is a shortcut to close the window.

To close a window with the mouse:

1. Click on the Control Menu box to display the Control menu.

2. Choose (click on) the Close command to close the window.

The "Quick Close" Using the Mouse To close a window with the mouse, simply double-click on the Control Menu box.

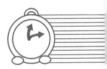

Quitting Windows If you double-click on the Program Manager's Control Menu box, you will exit Windows.

Moving Objects On-screen

You can also use the mouse to drag an object (usually a window, dialog box, or icon) to a new position on-screen.

Drag To drag an object to a new location on-screen, point to the object, hold down the left mouse button, and move the mouse to a new location. The object is dragged along with the mouse cursor.

Resizing a Window

You can also drag a window border to change the size of a window. Try dragging a window border. Point at the right-hand border of the Program Manager window.

The mouse pointer changes into a double-headed arrow. As you become more familiar with Windows and Windows applications, you will learn that the shape of the mouse pointer can tell you a lot. In this example, by changing into the double-headed arrow, the pointer is telling you that you can now drag the border to a new position.

Drag the window border to the left or right making the window smaller or larger. When the window is the desired size, release the mouse button. Dragging any one border allows you to increase or decrease the size of the window in only one direction.

Point the mouse pointer at the lower right corner of the Program Manager window. When the pointer is properly placed on the border corner, the pointer changes to a diagonal, double-headed arrow. Drag the border down and to the right. The border changes position as shown in Figure 2.1. When the window is the desired size, release the mouse button.

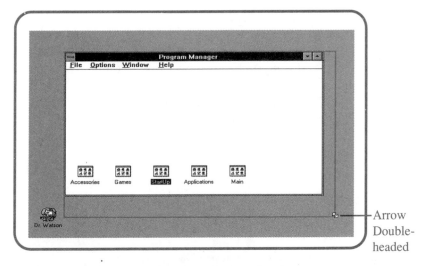

Arrow
Double-
headed

Figure 2.1   Dragging the window border.

Using Scroll Bars

Scroll bars appear when text, graphics, or icons in a window take up more space than the area shown. Using scroll bars, you can move up, down, left, or right in a window.

Figure 2.2 illustrates an example. If you drag the Applications icon outside the lower right of the Program Manager window area and release the mouse button. The scroll bars immediately appear. To use the scroll bars to view items outside the window, use the following technique:

1. To see an object that is down and to the right of the viewable area of the window, point at the down arrow located on the bottom of the vertical scroll bar.

2. Click on the arrow. The window's contents scroll up.

3. Click on the scroll arrow on the right side of the horizontal scroll bar. The window's contents move left.

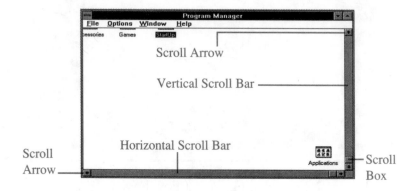

Figure 2.2 Scroll bars.

You can also drag the scroll box to move quickly to a distant area (top or bottom) of the window. To drag a scroll box:

1. Point to the scroll box in the scroll bar and hold down the mouse button.

2. Drag the scroll box to the new location.

3. Release the mouse button.

 **Window by Window**   You can move the contents of a window one windowful at a time. To do so, just click in the scroll bar on either side of the scroll box.

Empty Window?   Don't worry if text or graphics don't appear in a window. Use the scroll bars to bring the text or graphic into view.

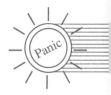

Navigating the Desktop with the Keyboard

In this lesson, you will learn how to use the keyboard to select objects and change the appearance of the screen.

More About Icons

An icon is a small picture in Windows that may represent:

- A document, directory, or disk drive.

- An application program (such as WordPerfect for Windows).

- A group of applications (such as Accessories).

Most icons have labels (some are more descriptive than others). Figure 3.1 shows the window which appears after opening the Games group icon. Notice that there are program-item icons for two games: Solitaire and Minesweeper. To play either game, open the appropriate icon.

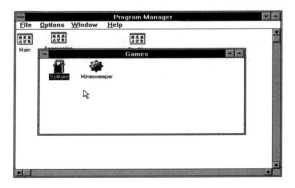

Figure 3.1   Game icons and their labels.

Opening an Icon into a Window

To open a group icon with the keyboard, follow these steps:

1. From the Program Manager window, press Ctrl-Tab as needed to select the group icon you want to open. The icon label appears highlighted when it's selected.

2. Press Enter to open the group window. See Figure 3.2.

3. Use the arrow keys to select the appropriate program-item icon within the group window.

4. Press Enter to open the program-item icon.

Active Window or Icon   The active window (or icon) is the one with the highlighted title bar (or label). Any commands you choose will affect the active window or icon. To use the keyboard, press Ctrl-Tab as often as is necessary to highlight the group window or group icon. Use the arrow keys to activate program-item icons within group windows.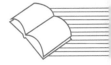

15

Application Window Control Menu Box

Group
Window
Control
Menu Box

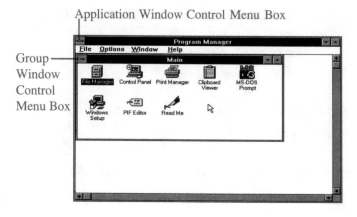

Figure 3.2 After opening the Main icon.

Closing a Window

To close the window with the keyboard:

1. Press Alt-hyphen to open the Control Menu (for group or file windows). If the window is an application window (i.e., Program Manager, Excel, etc.), use Alt-space bar to open the Control Menu.

2. Press C to choose the Close command to close the window.

The "Quick Close" Using the Keyboard To close a group or file window using the keyboard, press Ctrl-F4. If the window is an application window, press Alt-F4 to quit the application and close the window.

Refer to Figure 3.2 to locate the Control Menu box for the Main window. You could press Alt-hyphen to open the Control menu and press C to choose the Close option.

Moving or Resizing Windows with the Keyboard

You can use the keyboard to move and resize windows. These operations can be performed more quickly using the mouse, but you have more control using the keyboard. To use the keyboard to move a window to a new location on the screen:

1. Open the window's Control menu.

2. Press M to choose the **Move** command. The mouse pointer turns into a four-headed arrow (see Figure 3.3) positioned over the title bar.

3. Use the arrow keys to move the window to a new location.

4. Press Enter to accept the new location. Esc cancels the operation and returns the window to its original location.

Control Menu Options Unavailable   The Control Menu **M**ove and **S**ize commands are not active if the window is maximized. The **S**ize command is also unavailable if the window is minimized.

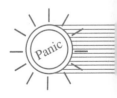

17

Active Window   Four-Headed Arrow Mouse Pointer

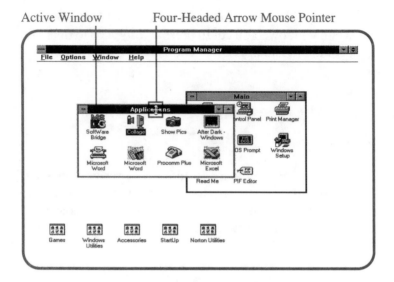

Figure 3.3   Moving a window using the keyboard.

To resize a window using the keyboard:

1. Open the window's Control menu.

2. Press S to choose the Size command. The mouse pointer will turn into a four-headed arrow.

3. Use the arrow keys to move the mouse pointer to the border or corner of the window you wish to resize. The four-headed arrow becomes a two-headed arrow, indicating the directions you can move the border.

4. Use the arrow keys to resize the window.

5. Press Enter to accept the new window size. Esc cancels the operation and returns the window to its original size.

In this lesson, you learned how to manipulate the Windows environment using the keyboard. In the next lesson, you'll learn how to make selections with the menus.

Lesson 4

Using Menus

In this lesson, you will learn how to select and open menus, choose menu commands, and how to quit Windows.

What Is a Menu?

A menu is a group of related commands from which you can choose a command to perform. Menus are organized in logical groups. For example, from the Program Manager window, all the commands related to files may be accessed via the File menu. The names of the menus available appear in the menu bar.

Menu Commands versus Shortcut Keys

When you first get started, you'll want to use the menus to view and select commands. Once you become more familiar with Windows, you'll probably want to use shortcut keys for often-used commands. They allow you to access a command without using the menus. Shortcut keys typically combine the Alt, Ctrl, or Shift key with a function key (such as F1). If a shortcut key is available, it will be listed on the pull-down menu, to the right of the command.

For example, Figure 4.1 shows the File menu from the Program Manager. You can choose File, Properties... to view the properties of a group or program-item icon, or press the shortcut key Alt-Enter to bypass the File menu.

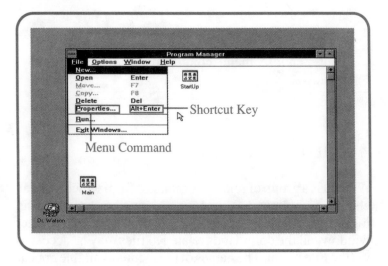

Figure 4.1   The Program Manager File menu.

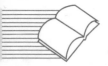 **Choosing Menu Commands**   This book uses the format *menu title, menu command* to tell you what menu commands to choose. In the above example, "choose File, Properties..." is equivalent to "open the File menu and select the Properties... command."

Choosing Menu Commands with the Mouse

You can choose a menu command with the mouse or the keyboard. To use the mouse, click on the menu title in the menu bar. The menu opens to display the available commands. To choose a particular command, click on it with the mouse pointer.

Here's an example. To see the **Help** options available for the Program Manager, just click on the Help menu title in the Program Manager menu bar (see Figure 4.2).

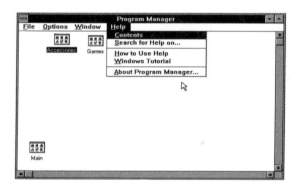

Figure 4.2   The Help menu.

To see the contents of the Program Manager Help facility, choose Contents. The Program Manager Help window shown in Figure 4.3 appears. Notice that when the mouse pointer is positioned over a specific Help topic, it becomes a pointing finger. You can move the finger to any option and click on that option for specific Help information. (Remember, to close this or any window, double-click on the Control Menu box.)

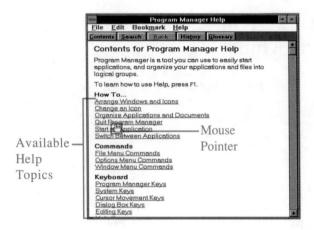

Figure 4.3   The Program Manager Help window.

Choosing Menu Commands Using the Keyboard

You can also select menus with the keyboard. Press Alt to activate the menu bar of the active window. Notice that the first menu title becomes highlighted. Once the menu bar is active, you may choose between two methods to select a menu:

- Use the arrow keys to highlight the menu title you want and press Enter.

- Press the underlined letter of the menu. (For example, to open the **H**elp menu, you would press H.)

To open the Control Menu with the keyboard, press Alt-space bar if the window is an application window (such as Microsoft Word or Program Manager) or Alt-hyphen if the window is a document or group window. You can then highlight your selection using the arrow keys and press Enter, or you can press the underlined letter of the command.

Commands, Options, or Selections? Commands, menu options, and menu selections all refer to the same thing—items you choose from a menu. Further, commands may be "performed," "executed," or "selected." This simply means that the computer carries out the instructions associated with the command (whether it is to display another menu or perform an operation).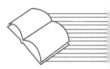

To close the Control menu (or any menu for that matter), press Esc.

Reading a Menu

Common conventions are used throughout Windows menus. Figure 4.4 illustrates the Program Manager File menu. Selection letters (letters you press to choose a command) are underlined. Also, shortcut keys (where available) are listed to the right of the command. Use these to bypass menus.

Unavailable Commands Some commands may appear grayed-out. These commands can only be used under certain circumstances. For example, you cannot copy an icon before you first select one to be copied.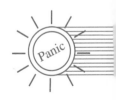

Another menu convention shown in Figure 4.4 is the use of the ellipsis (...) after a command. The ellipsis indicates that more information is needed before the command is completed. Windows usually employs a *dialog box* to gather this information from you. For more on dialog boxes, see Lesson 5.

Highlighted Command

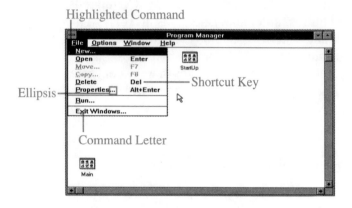

Ellipsis

Shortcut Key

Command Letter

Figure 4.4   The Program Manager File menu.

For example, suppose you want to exit Windows. Follow these steps. (Notice the ellipsis following the **Exit Windows** command.)

1. Open the File menu using either the mouse or the keyboard.

2. Choose Exit Windows.... A dialog box appears.

3. If you want to exit Windows, click on the OK command button or press Enter. To abort the exit process, click on the Cancel command button or press Esc.

Another common menu symbol is the check mark. The check mark indicates that a menu option is currently active. Each time you choose the menu command, the option is turned on or off (like a light switch).

Lesson 5

Using Dialog Boxes

In this lesson, you will learn how to use dialog boxes to access and enter information.

What is a Dialog Box?

Windows uses dialog boxes to exchange information with you. Most often, dialog boxes ask you to provide more information so that an operation can be completed. A menu command followed by an ellipsis (...) indicates that a dialog box will be used to gather more information. Dialog boxes are often used to warn you about a problem (for example, `File already exists, Overwrite?`) or confirm that an operation should take place (for example, the Exit Windows dialog box).

Components of a Dialog Box

Dialog boxes vary in complexity. Some ask you to confirm an operation before it is executed—for example, a dialog box that asks you if you want to format a disk. In this case, you would select OK to confirm or Cancel to abort the operation. Other dialog boxes are quite complex, asking you to specify several options.

The following list briefly explains the components of a dialog box. The following sections describe the components and how to use them in greater detail.

Text Box   A text box allows you to type in an entry, for example, a name for a file you want to save or a label for an icon you've just added to a group.

List Box   A list box presents a list of possible choices from which you may choose. Scroll bars often allow you to scroll through the list. Often, a text box is associated with a list box. The list item that you select appears in the text box associated with the list.

Drop-Down List Box   A single-line list box that opens to display a list of choices when you click on the down-arrow button on the right side of the list box.

Option Buttons   Option buttons present a group of related choices from which you may choose one. Option buttons are sometimes (and incorrectly) referred to as radio buttons.

Check Boxes   Check boxes present a single option or group of related options. The command option is active if an x appears in the box next to it.

Command Buttons   Command buttons carry out the command displayed on the button (Open, Quit, Cancel, OK, and so on). If there is an ellipsis on the button, choosing it will open another dialog box (Options...).

Text Box

A text box allows you to enter information needed to complete a command. This is typically a file name or directory name. Figure 5.1 displays the Move dialog box (accessed from the File Manager File menu).

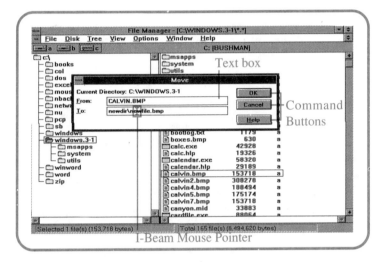

Figure 5.1   The Move dialog box from the Windows File Manager.

To activate a text box using the mouse:

1. Point at the text box you wish to activate. Notice that the mouse pointer changes to an I-beam when you point at the text box.

2. Click the left mouse button to activate the text box.

To activate a text box using the keyboard:

• Use the selection key sequence to activate the text box. For example, to activate the **T**o: text box in Figure 5.1, press Alt-T.

27

Once you have activated a text box, you can use several keys to edit the text you enter. Table 5.1 outlines these keys.

Table 5.1 Editing keys for text boxes

Key	Description
Del	Deletes the character to the right of the insertion point.
Backspace	Erases the character to the left of the insertion point.
End	Moves the insertion point to the end of the line.
Home	Moves the insertion point to the beginning of the line.
Arrow keys	Moves the insertion point one character in the direction of the arrow.
Shift-End	Selects the text from the insertion point to the end of the line.
Shift-Home	Selects the text from the insertion point to the beginning of the line.
Shift-Arrow	Selects the next character in the direction of the arrow.
Ctrl-Ins	Copies selected text.
Shift-Ins	Pastes selected text.

List Boxes

A list box is designed to allow you to make a selection from a list of available options. For example, the list box displayed in the Browse dialog box (shown in Figure 5.2) allows you to select a file to open.

Linked Text Box   List Box Scroll Bar

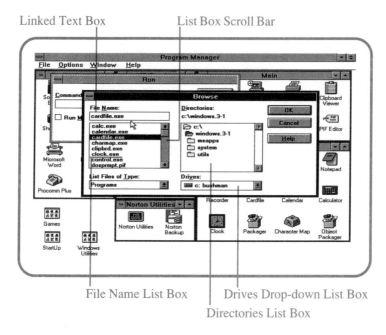

File Name List Box | Drives Drop-down List Box
                    Directories List Box

Figure 5.2   The Browse dialog box.

Notice the scroll bar along the right-hand side of the list box displayed in Figure 5.2. You can use the scroll bar to bring items in the list into view.

To select an item from a list box using the mouse, click on the appropriate list item. Notice that in the Browse list box, the item you select is automatically displayed in the linked text box above the list box. Press Enter or click on OK to accept the selection, press Esc or click on Cancel to close the dialog box without making the selection.

To select an item from a list box using the keyboard:

1. Use Alt-selection letter to activate the list box. For example, to activate the File Name list box displayed in Figure 5.2, press Alt-N.

2. Use ↑ and ↓ or PageUp and PageDown to move through the list. Each list item will become highlighted as you come to it.

3. Press Enter to accept the selection and close the dialog box.

To select an item from a drop-down list box using the mouse, open the list box by clicking on the down-arrow button and then click on the appropriate list item. To select a drop-down list box item using the keyboard:

1. Use Alt-selection letter to activate the list box.

2. Use ↓ to open the drop-down list box.

3. Use ↑ and ↓ or PageUp and PageDown to scroll through the list.

4. Press Enter to make your selection and close the dialog box.

Option Buttons

Option buttons allow you to make a single choice from a list of possible command options. For example, the Print Range options displayed in Figure 5.3 allow you to select which pages of your document to print. The active option is indicated by the small, filled-in circle (the **All** option in Figure 5.3 is currently active).

To select an option button with the mouse, click on the circle for the option you want. To use the keyboard, press Alt plus the selection letter for the option you want. For example, press Alt-A to activate the **All** option in Figure 5.3.

Print Range
Option
Buttons

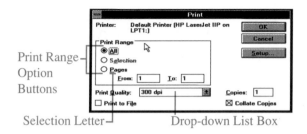

Selection Letter

Drop-down List Box

Figure 5.3 The Print dialog box from Windows Write.

Check Boxes

Command options you can select (activate) or deselect (deactivate) are usually presented as check boxes. When a check box is selected, an X appears in the box, and the associated command option is active (see Figure 5.4).

To select or deselect a check box option, click on its box with the mouse pointer. To use the keyboard, press Alt-*selection letter* to select or deselect a check box. For example, press Alt-S to activate the System option in Figure 5.4.

Command Buttons

Command buttons are used to perform operations. In Figure 5.4, three common command buttons appear. The OK command button is used to accept the information you have entered or verify an action and close the dialog box. Pressing Enter is equivalent to selecting the OK button. Cancel is used to leave the dialog box without executing the information you provided in the dialog box. Pressing Esc is the keyboard equivalent to selecting the Cancel button.

Help is another common command button that provides you help specific to the dialog box you are working in. Alt-H and F1 are the keyboard equivalents to selecting the **H**elp button.

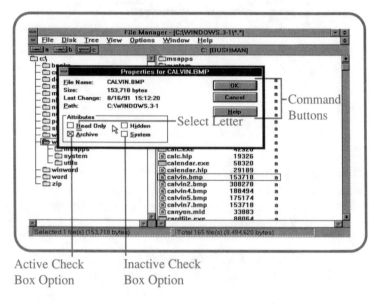

Active Check   Inactive Check
Box Option   Box Option

Figure 5.4 The Properties dialog box from the Windows File Manager.

Accidents Happen If you accidently select the Cancel command button, don't worry. You can always reenter the dialog box and continue. Be careful when you select OK. The instructions you have entered in the dialog box are executed.

In this lesson, you learned how to use dialog boxes. In the next lesson you will earn how to exit Windows and, perhaps more importantly, what to do before you exit.

Lesson 6

Exiting Windows

So far, you have learned several ways to exit Windows. In this lesson, you will learn the steps to take before you leave Windows as well as other ways to exit Windows.

Methods to Exit Windows

Three methods are available to quit Windows:

- Through the Program Manager File menu.

- Through the Program Manager Control menu.

- With a shortcut key.

Exit Using the File Menu

You may exit Windows using the File menu (see Figure 6.1).

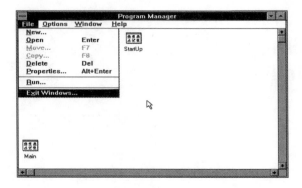

Figure 6.1 Using the File menu to exit Windows.

To use the mouse, follow these steps:

1. Choose File, Exit Windows from the Program Manager window.

2. Exit Windows by selecting the OK command button in the Exit Windows dialog box.

To use the keyboard, follow these steps:

1. Press Alt to activate the Program Manager menu bar.

2. Open File by pressing F or Enter.

3. Select Exit Windows by pressing X or use ↓ to highlight Exit Windows and press Enter. The Exit Windows dialog box appears, as shown in Figure 6.2.

4. Exit Windows by selecting the OK command button in the Exit Windows dialog box.

Figure 6.2   The Exit Windows dialog box.

Exit Using the Control Menu

To exit Windows using the Control menu, double-click the Program Manager Control Menu box. If you prefer to use the keyboard (see Figure 6.3), follow these steps:

1. Press Alt-space bar to open the Program Manager Control menu.

2. Select Close by pressing C or use ↓ to highlight Close and press Enter.

3. Exit Windows by selecting the OK command button in the Exit Windows dialog box.

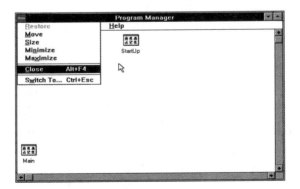

Figure 6.3   Using the Control menu to exit Windows.

35

Exit Using a Shortcut Key

As you may have noticed in Figure 6.3, a shortcut key is available to exit Windows. Once you have closed any open documents and applications and returned to the Program Manager window, press Alt-F4.

Windows Protects You

Because you can work with several documents and applications at one time, you may get carried away and forget to save a document before you exit Windows. Fear not; Windows protects you. For example, if you're working on a Write document and try to exit Windows without saving the document, the dialog box shown in Figure 6.4 prompts you to save your changes.

Figure 6.4   The Write: Save Current Changes? dialog box.

Select Yes to save the changes, No to discard any changes you made, or Cancel to stop exiting Windows. This dialog box helps you avoid losing document changes.

Forget To Save?   This message is your only warning. If you accidently respond No to saving current changes, the changes made in the document are lost.

Leaving Applications Before Exiting Windows

Even though Windows provides the protection described, it is safest to get in the habit of closing documents and applications yourself before quitting Windows.

In most Windows applications, Choose File, Save to save a document. Then, exit the application. If it is a Windows application, you can exit just as you would exit Windows (press Alt-F4 or choose File, Exit).

The Way Things Were

If you've made any changes to the Program Manager window during your Windows session, you may want to save them so they will appear the next time you start Windows. The changes might include moving icons around within group windows, moving windows around within the Program Manager window, or even changing which windows will be open when you next start Windows.

To activate this option using the mouse, choose Options, Save Settings on Exit. A check mark appears when this option is active. To use the keyboard, from the Program Manager window:

1. Press Alt to activate the menu bar.

2. Press O to open the Options menu.

3. Press S to activate the Save Settings on Exit command.

Save A Step   If you want a particular application to start automatically every time you start Windows, place its program-item icon in the Program Manager group named StartUp.

Starting and Exiting Applications

In this lesson, you will learn how to start and exit Windows applications.

Starting Windows Applications

A Windows application is a program designed to take advantage of the Graphical User Interface built into Windows. By definition, a GUI provides a common interface between you and your programs. In the context of this lesson, this means that you are able to start (and exit) most Windows applications using the same procedures. If you are using a non-Windows (DOS) application through Windows, you will need to consult the manual for that application to learn how to start and exit.

There are several ways to start a Windows application; two that are discussed in this chapter are:

- Using the program-item icon associated with the application.

- Using the Program Manager **F**ile, **R**un command.

In Lesson 17, you will learn how to use the File Manager to start an application.

Using the Application Icon

You most often will use the program-item icon to start an application. When a Windows application is added to a Program Manager group, a program-item icon for the application is created. To use the program-item icon to open the application, you must first locate it in one of the Program Manager's groups. For example, if you want to use Write, you would need to open the Accessories group icon to access the Write program-item icon. Figure 7.1 shows the Accessories group window and the program-item icons that might appear in it.

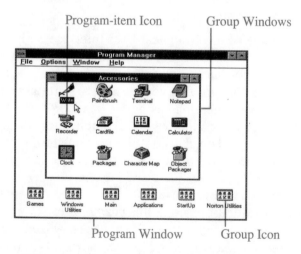

Figure 7.1 Program-item icons in the Accessories group.

To use the mouse to start an application from the program-item icon, follow these steps:

1. Open (double-click on) the Program Manager group that contains the program-item icon for the application you want to use.

2. Double click on the program-item icon for the application. The application window appears.

   To start an application using the keyboard:

1. From the Program Manager window, press Ctrl-Tab to highlight the desired program group icon.

2. Press Enter to open the group window.

3. Use the arrow keys to highlight the program-item icon for the application you want to use.

4. Press Enter to start the application. The application window appears.

Using the Run Command

You can also use the Program Manager File, **R**un command to start applications. Using the **R**un command allows you to enter command parameters or options that change the way the application is started. For example, most word processors can be started so that a file you specify is automatically opened and ready to edit. Figure 7.2 displays the command that will open WordPerfect for Windows (wpwin) with a file (report.wpp) open and ready to edit. If necessary, you can include the path statement (drive and directory) for the program file and/or the document file.

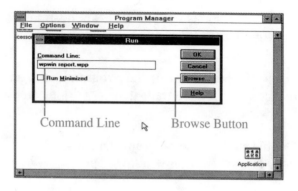

Figure 7.2 Loading WordPerfect for Windows and a document file using the Windows File, Run command.

What Are Your Options? Check the documentation that comes with your software for the start-up options available. You may want to jot down special start-up commands you plan on using often.

To use the **R**un command, follow these steps:

1. From the Program Manager window, choose File, Run. The Run command dialog box appears (see Figure 7.3).

2. Type the command in text box. Examples of possible commands are as follows:

```
WPWIN
C:\WPWIN\WPWIN
C:\WPWIN\WPWIN REPORT.WPP
C:\WPWIN\WPWIN C:\MYFILES\REPORT.WPP
```

3. When the command is complete, select OK. (If you decide not to use the **R**un command, select Cancel.)

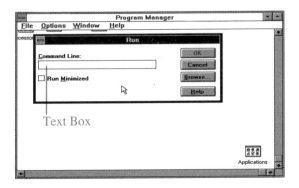

Figure 7.3   The Run dialog box ready for your command.

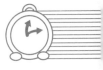

If You Don't Remember the Command   Suppose you don't remember the command that will run the application. There are two routes to a solution. The most direct route is to use the **B**rowse button on the Run dialog box. The Browse dialog box shown in Figure 7.4 appears. From it, you can see files which may be selected. Or you may select files to run from the File Manager (see Lesson 17).

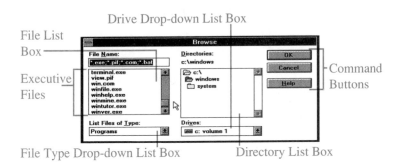

Figure 7.4   The Browse dialog box.

Using a Document Window

When you use specific applications with Windows, you will create documents. For example, a letter you create with WordPerfect for Windows will be contained in a document. These documents are sometimes called files or document files. When you are working on a document, it appears in a window.

Creating and Opening a Document Window

When you start up an application, a window for a new document is created for you. If you want to create another document window, you may choose the **File, New** command from that application's menu bar. A new window is created for you to start a new document and the document you were working on is still available.

Save Your Work   Always save your documents using the **File, Save** command. You should give each document file a unique name. That way, you can use the **File, Open** command later to open the document file and continue working.

Closing a Document Window

When you are done with a document, always save your changes and close the document window. Choose File, Save and then choose File, Exit, or simply double-click on the Control Menu box. This ensures the document will not be lost or damaged accidently.

Exiting Windows Applications

Before you exit an application, make sure the open documents for that application are saved and closed through the File menu.

Forget to Save Your Changes? If you attempt to close a document window or exit an application before you save changes, Windows will ask you if you want to save before closing. (See Figure 7.5 for an example.) This is a safety feature built into Windows. To save your work, click on the Yes command button. To exit without saving your work, click on the No command button. To remain in the application, click on the Cancel command button.

Figure 7.5   The Write: Save Changes? dialog box.

There are three ways to exit a Windows application:

- With the Control menu.

- With the application's Exit command.

- With the shortcut key.

Close or Exit? The term *close* is used in reference to document windows. When you are finished working on a document, save your changes and close the document window. The application will still be open. The Exit command will close your document window(s) *and* exit the application.

Using the Application Control Menu

To exit an application using its Control menu, double-click on the Control Menu box. If you prefer the keyboard:

1. Press Alt-space bar to open the Applications Control menu.

2. Press C to choose the Close command.

Using the Application's Exit Command

You may exit an application by choosing File, Exit. You can click on the commands with the mouse or press Alt to activate the menu bar and proceed with the keyboard.

Using the Shortcut Key

The quick route to exiting is to use the shortcut key. Press Alt-F4 and you're on your way.

In this lesson, you learned how to start and exit applications, and you learned common methods for creating, saving, and exiting a document window. In the next lesson, you will learn how to resize and move windows.

Lesson 8
Resizing and Moving Windows

In this lesson, you will learn more about moving windows and changing their size.

Sizing with Maximize, Minimize, and Restore

You may want to increase the size of a window to see its full contents. Or, you may want to decrease the size (even down to icon form) to make room for other windows. One way to resize a window is to use the Maximize, Minimize, and Restore commands. If you use the mouse, you will use the Maximize, Minimize and Restore buttons located on the right side of the window title bar. If you use the keyboard, you can use the menu commands through the Control menu. Table 8.1 displays the Maximize, Minimize, and Restore buttons and defines the purpose of each one.

Figure 8.1 shows the Program Manager window maximized to full-screen size. At full size, the minimize and restore buttons are available. Figure 8.2 displays the Program Manager window with the Minimize and Maximize buttons.

Table 8.1 Window Sizing Command Buttons

Command Button	Description
▲	Select the Maximize button to enlarge the window to its maximum size.
▼	Select the Minimize button to reduce the Window to its icon form.
⬍	The Restore button is only available after a window has been maximized. Select it to return a window to the size it was before it was maximized.

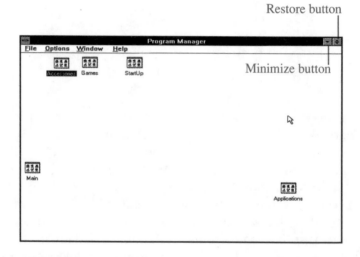

Restore button

Minimize button

Figure 8.1 The Program Manager window maximized to full-screen size.

To maximize, minimize, or restore a window with the mouse, click on the appropriate button. To maximize, minimize, or restore a window with the keyboard, follow these steps:

1. Open the window's Control menu (see Figure 8.3).

2. Select the Restore, Minimize, or Maximize command from the menu.

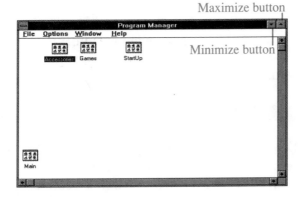

Figure 8.2   Program Manager window at regular size.

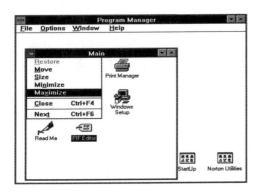

Figure 8.3   The Main group window Control menu.

Can't Choose Restore? Remember that some menu items will not be available under certain circumstances. Notice that the **R**estore command is unavailable (grayed-out) in Figure 8.3. This is because the window is not maximized.

Sizing the Borders

A particular size of window may be required to suit your needs. If so, simply drag the window border to change the size of the window. This may be done with the mouse or the keyboard.

To use the mouse, follow these steps:

1. Place the mouse pointer on the portion of the border (vertical, horizontal, or corner) that you want to resize. When the mouse pointer is positioned correctly, it will change into one of the shapes displayed in Table 8.2.

2. Drag the border to the new position. A faint line appears where the border will be when you release the mouse button.

3. Once the border is in the desired location, release the mouse button. The window is resized.

To resize a window using the keyboard, follow these steps:

1. Open the window's Control menu (press Alt-space bar or Alt-hyphen.)

2. Press S to choose the **S**ize command. The pointer becomes a four-headed arrow.

3. Use the arrow keys to move the pointer to the border or corner you wish to resize. The mouse pointer turns into one of the shapes displayed in Table 8.2.

4. With the pointer on the border or corner, press the arrow keys to resize the window. A faint line appears showing the new border location.

5. When the faint lines show the sizing you want, press Enter. To cancel the operation, press Esc.

Table 8.2   Window Resizing Mouse Pointers

Mouse Pointer	Description
⇕	The vertical double-headed arrow appears when you position the mouse pointer over either the top or bottom window border. It allows you to resize the window by dragging the border up or down.
⇔	The horizontal double-headed arrow appears when you position the mouse pointer over either side of the window border. It allows you to resize the window by dragging the border left or right.
⤡	The diagonal double-headed arrow appears when you position the mouse pointer over any of the four corners of the window border. It allows you to resize the window by dragging the corner diagonally.

Missing Some Icons?   When you reduce the size of a window, some of the contents may not be visible in the resulting window size. Remember that you can use the scroll bars to see the contents of the window.

51

Moving a Window

When you start working with multiple windows, moving a window becomes as important as sizing one. You will want to move windows to make room for other work on your desktop. You may move a window with the mouse or keyboard.

To move a window using the mouse, point at the Window's title bar and drag it to a new location. To use the keyboard:

1. Open the window Control menu (press Alt-space bar or Alt-hyphen).

2. Press M to choose the **M**ove command. The pointer will appear as a four-headed arrow.

3. Use the arrow keys to move the window to a new location.

4. When the window is in the new location, press Enter. To cancel the operation and return the window to its original location, press Esc.

In this lesson, you learned how to change the appearance of your desktop by changing the size of or moving a window. In the next lesson, you will learn how to open, arrange, and move among multiple windows.

Lesson 9
Working with Multiple Windows

In this lesson, you will learn how to open and arrange multiple windows. You will also learn how to move between windows.

Multiple Windows

Windows allows you to use more than one application at a time, and each Windows application supports multiple document windows. As you can imagine, opening multiple applications with multiple windows can make your desktop pretty busy! That's why it's important to be able to arrange and switch between windows easily.

As you learned in Lesson 7, you can open a program-item window by double-clicking on the icon or using the **Run** command. To open a new document window within an application, choose the File, New command associated with the application.

Arranging Windows

Once you have multiple open windows, you can use the commands under the **Window** menu to arrange the

53

windows. Figure 9.1 shows several windows open at the same time. These are windows created from the group icons on the Program Manager screen, but they could be various program-item or document windows as well. The screen is confusing and, as you'll see, one window is hidden by the others.

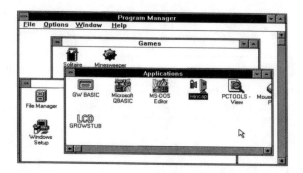

Figure 9.1 The Program manager with multiple windows open.

Cascading Windows

A good way to get control of a confusing desktop is to choose the Window, Cascade command. Choosing this command causes Windows to lay all the open windows on top of each other so the title bar of each is visible. The resulting cascaded window arrangement is shown in Figure 9.2.

Cascade Quickly Press the shortcut key combination Shift-F5 to cascade your windows without using the Window menu.

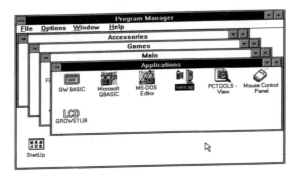

Figure 9.2 The windows after selecting Window, Cascade.

Tiling Windows

Another arrangement is referred to as *tiled*. When you choose this command, Windows resizes and moves each open window so they appear side-by-side. Choose Window, Tile and an arrangement similar to that shown in Figure 9.3 appears.

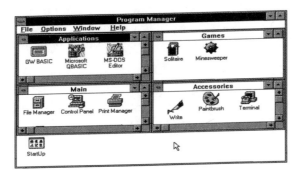

Figure 9.3 The windows after selecting Window, Tile.

Timely Tiling   Press the shortcut key combination Shift-F4 to cascade your windows without using the **W**indow menu.

Arranging Icons

Another **W**indow command is **A**rrange Icons. This command is handy after you move icons out of your way by dragging them with the mouse. When things get confusing, choose **W**indow, **A**rrange Icons to clean up after yourself.

Instead of Using the Scroll Bars   If you make a window smaller and can no longer see all the icons in the window, select Window, Arrange Icons to bring the icons into the new, smaller window area.

Moving Between Windows

Another common dilemma when using multiple windows is how to move between windows. The application (and document window if available) currently in use has a highlighted title bar. That's how you know which window is active.

Now Where Was I?   The window currently in use is called the active window. Moving to a new window means you are changing the window that is active.

If you are using a mouse, click on any part of the window you want to use (make active). The title bar is highlighted, and you may work in the window.

To use the keyboard, open the **W**indow menu by pressing Alt-W. Figure 9.4 shows the Program Manager's **W**indow menu. Notice that the available windows appear in a numbered list. Simply press the number next to the window title you wish to activate. Most Windows applications make use of the **W**indow menu.

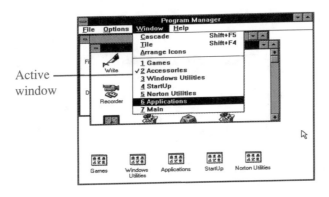

Figure 9.4   The Program Manager's **W**indow menu.

Make sure you are able to move between windows before proceeding.

Moving Between Applications

Remember that Windows allows you to have multiple windows open within an application *and* have multiple applications open at the same time. The last section taught you how to move between windows in the same application. This section will tell you how to move between applications.

Using the Task List

A dialog box called the Task List can be used to switch between applications. A sample Task List is shown in Figure 9.5. There are three applications running. Notice that the entry for Write (Windows' word processor application) is followed by the name of the active document window (RPT2.WRI).

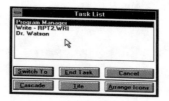

Figure 9.5 The Task List with three running applications.

To use the mouse to switch applications using the Task List, follow these steps:

1. Click on the Control Menu box. The Control menu appears.

2. Click on the Switch To command. The Task List appears.

3. Highlight the application to switch to by clicking it on.

4. Click on the Switch To button and you are taken to the application.

The keyboard can also be used with the Task List. These are the steps:

1. Press Ctrl-Esc to display the Task List.

2. Press ↑ or ↓ until the application you want is high-lighted.

3. Press Enter.

Bypass the Task List Hold down the Alt key and press the Tab key. (Keep the Alt key down.) A dialog box appears displaying the name of one of the open applications. Each time you press the Tab key, a new (open) application is displayed. When you see the application you want, release the Alt key and you will switch to that application. If you decide you don't want to switch task after all, press Esc and release the Alt key. This technique works with both Windows and non-Windows applications.

In this lesson, you learned how to control your desktop by opening and arranging windows. You also learned how to move between multiple windows and applications. In the next lesson, you will learn how to move information between windows with the **Cut, Copy,** and **Paste** commands.

Lesson 10

Copy, Cut, and Paste Text Between Windows

In this lesson, you will learn how to move information between windows using Copy, Cut, and Paste in conjunction with the Clipboard.

What Is the Clipboard?

One of the handiest features of the Windows environment is that information (both text and graphics) can be copied or moved from one window to another. This includes windows (documents) in the same application as well as between applications. When information is copied or cut, it is placed in an area called the Clipboard.

The Clipboard holds only the most recent information copied or cut. When you copy or cut something else, it replaces what was previously on the Clipboard.

Cut, Copy, and Paste When you *cut* information, it is removed from its original location and placed on the Clipboard. When you *copy* information, it is copied to the Clipboard without disturbing the original. When you *paste*, the information on the Clipboard is duplicated at the location you specify, without disturbing the copy on the Clipboard.

60

You can see the contents of the Clipboard at any time by following these steps:

1. Open the Main group icon.

2. From the Main window, open the Clipboard Viewer program-item icon.

3. The contents of the Clipboard appears in the Clipboard Viewer window. In Figure 10.1, an address was copied or cut to the Clipboard.

Figure 10.1   The contents of the Clipboard seen through the Clipboard Viewer.

Without a Trace   When you turn off your computer or exit Windows, the contents of the Clipboard is lost.

Take a look at the contents of your Clipboard. Unless you have recently cut or copied information, the Clipboard will be empty.

Selecting Text

Before you can cut or copy text, you must identify which text is to be cut or copied. This is called *selecting* text.

Selected text is highlighted so you can quickly distinguish it. Figure 10.2 illustrates selected text in a Write document.

Selected Text

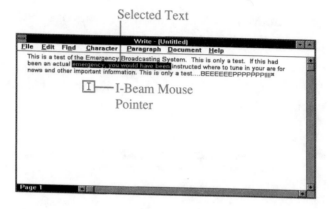

Figure 10.2   Selected text in a Write document.

To select text with the mouse:

1. Position the I-beam pointer just before the first character to be selected.

2. Hold down the left mouse button and drag the I-beam pointer to the last character to be selected.

3. Release the mouse button. The selected text is highlighted.

To select text with the keyboard:

1. Use the arrow keys to position the insertion point (blinking vertical line) just before the first character to be selected.

2. Hold down the Shift key and use the arrow keys to move the highlight to the last character to be selected.

3. Release all keys. The selected text is highlighted.

Deselecting Text   To get rid of the highlight on the selection, click anywhere in the document with the mouse. To get rid of the highlight with the keyboard, press an arrow key.

Text Selection Shortcuts   To select a single word using the mouse, double-click on the word. To select text word-by-word (instead of character-by-character), hold down both the Shift and Ctrl keys while using the arrow keys.

Selecting Graphics

The procedure for selecting graphics depends on the Windows application program you are using. In a word processing program such as Write, graphics are selected the same way as text. In a program like Paintbrush, there are special tools for cutting and copying either rectangular or irregular shapes. Since the procedure varies, it is best to refer to the documentation for each application.

Using Copy, Cut, and Paste Between Windows

Once you have selected the text or graphics, the procedures for cutting, copying, and pasting are the same in all

Windows applications. To cut or copy and paste information between windows of the same application as well as between windows of different applications:

1. Select the text or graphic to cut or copy (following the instructions earlier in this lesson).

2. Open the Edit menu.

3. Choose Edit, Copy to keep the original selection in place or Cut to remove the original selection. The selected material is placed in the Clipboard.

4. Position the I-beam or insertion point where you want to insert the selection. (You may need to open another application or document.)

5. Open the Edit menu.

6. Choose Edit, Paste. The selection is copied from the Clipboard to your document. A copy remains on the Clipboard until you cut or copy something else.

Multiple Copies   Because items remain on the Clipboard until you cut or copy again, you can paste information from the Clipboard multiple times. You can also perform other tasks before you paste.

Try it. Enter your address in Write and select it. Choose Edit, Copy to copy it to the Clipboard. Choose File, New to open a new Write window. Then, choose Edit, Paste to paste the address in the new window. When you're done, choose File, Exit to exit the Write program.

Lesson 11

Managing Programs with the Program Manager

In this lesson, you will learn about groups and how they keep track of your applications. You'll learn how to add new groups and new program-item icons to those groups, delete groups and program-item icons you don't need, and move program-item icons from group to group.

What Is a Group?

Imagine how it would be if all the icons for all of your programs were contained in one group window. You would have to search through them all every time you wanted to run a program! Luckily, Windows offers groups to help organize the program-item icons into logical categories.

A group is a window within the Program Manager window. When it's closed, it appears as a group icon on the desktop; when it's open, it reveals program-item icons for various applications you can run.

Windows sets up several useful groups for you automatically, such as Accessories, Main, and Games. You are not stuck with just these, however; you can create your own groups, move program-item icons to different groups, delete icons, and even delete groups.

Creating a Group

As you begin to use Windows, you may find that you want additional groups. For example, if there are a few applications that you use every day, you may want to set up a group for them. You may also wish to create separate groups for Windows and non-Windows applications.

To create a group, follow these steps:

1. From the Program Manager windows, choose File, New. The New Program Object dialog box appears (see Figure 11.1).

2. Make sure Program Group is selected.

3. Select OK. The Program Group Properties dialog box appears.

4. Type the Description (which will become the group icon label and the group window title).

5. Select OK. The group window is now created. A window with the description you entered appears.

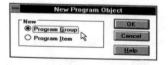

Figure 11.1   The New Program Object dialog box.

Try creating a group window for your own application. Once the group window is created, you can either drag applications into it from other groups or add applications by choosing File, New.

Adding an Application to a Group

Applications Must Be Installed   Adding an application to a group is *not* the same as installing the application on your computer. The application must already be installed on your computer before you can add it to a group.

Adding an application to a group links the execution of the application to a program-item icon displayed in the group. When you add an application to a group, you really do two things:

- Set up a program-item icon to launch the application.

- Tell Windows what file to execute when the icon is opened.

Applications may be added to any group, including the ones that were created when Windows was installed. Follow these steps:

1. Open the group window that you want the new program-item icon to reside in.

2. From the Program Manager, choose File, New. The New Program Object dialog box appears.

3. Select the Program Item option button and then select OK. The Program Item Properties dialog box appears (see Figure 11.2).

4. Enter a Description for the icon. This description will appear as the icon label and the group window title.

5. Enter the Command Line to the executable file including the path. For example, if you're adding WordPerfect 5.1 from the C:\WP51 directory, enter `C:\WP51\WP.EXE`.

What's an Executable File? The *executable file* is the file name you normally type at the DOS prompt to start the application. If you don't know what it is, look in the application's documentation. Executable files usually end in .EXE. You can select the Browse command button to open the Browse dialog box. From here, you can search for and select the executable file you want included as the Command line.

6. If you want a different default directory while you're running the application, enter a **W**orking Directory. In most cases, you can skip this step.

7. To start the application as a desktop icon (instead of in a window), check **R**un Minimized.

8. Select OK when the Program Item Properties dialog box is complete.

Figure 11.2 illustrates a completed Program Item Properties dialog box. This is to set up an application called Collage Plus Version 3.2 within the Screen Utilities group.

Figure 11.2 The Completed Program Item Properties dialog box.

Figure 11.3 shows the Screen Utilities group window with the program-item icon just created. In this case, the icon was supplied by the application manufacturer, and referenced in the COLLAGE.EXE file. If an icon is not found by Windows, it assigns an icon for you.

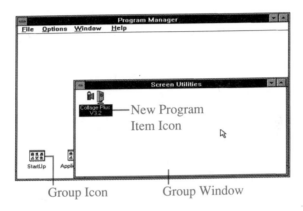

Group Icon   Group Window

Figure 11.3   The Screen Utilities group window with the Collage Plus program-item icon.

Changing Icons   If you don't like the looks of a program-item icon, you can assign a different one to the application. Choose File, Properties... from the Program Manager window. Select the Change Icon... command button and specify a new icon file. Windows 3.1 provides a host of new icons; the file MORICONS.DLL in the Windows directory contains these icons.

After you have added an application, test it by double-clicking on the program-item icon to run the application. If it works, you're ready to move on. If it doesn't, Windows will tell you what is wrong. Go back and try the steps again, making sure that the path and executable file name are correct.

69

Deleting an Application from a Group

In rearranging the groups to best meet your needs, you may want to delete an application from a group. For example, if your system doesn't have any sound recording or playback capabilities, you may want to delete the Sound Recorder application that Windows installed in the Accessories group.

What Am I Really Deleting?   Deleting an application from a group does not remove that application from your computer—it just makes Windows forget that it's there. Should you ever need to run it through Windows, you can add the application again using the steps you learned earlier in this lesson or simply run it from the File Manager (see Lesson 17).

To delete a program-item icon for an application from a group, follow these steps:

1. Open the group window.

2. Select the program-item icon for the application you wish to delete.

3. From the Program Manager, choose File, Delete. A message appears asking you to confirm the deletion (see Figure 11-4).

4. Select Yes to delete the application or No to cancel.

Figure 11.4 The Delete Program-Item Icon confirmation dialog box.

Deleting a Group

You can also delete a whole group and all its associated program-item icons. When you do, the program files related to those program-items remain on your computer—Windows just forgets where they are located.

To delete a group, follow these steps:

1. From the Program Manager screen, select the group icon you wish to delete.

2. Choose File, Delete. A message (similar to Figure 11.4) appears asking for confirmation.

3. Select Yes to delete the group or No to cancel.

In this lesson, you learned how to control access to the software installed on your computer through the addition of groups and program-item icons. You also learned how to delete both program-item icons and groups. In the next lesson, you'll learn how to view drives and directories with the File Manager.

Viewing Drives and Directories with the File Manager

In this lesson, you will learn to control disk drives and directories with the File Manager. You'll learn some basics about drives, directories, and files, and you'll learn how to manipulate them through the File Manager program.

What Are Drives?

A *drive* is the hardware that makes a disk function (seek, read, and write). A hard disk and its drive are considered one inseparable unit, while a floppy disk can easily be removed from its drive and replaced with a different disk.

Drives are given letter names. Drives A and B for most computers are floppy disk drives, used to store and retrieve data from diskettes. The designation for the hard disk inside the computer is typically drive C. (Since hard disks and their drives are not easily separated, the terms *disk* and *drive* are often used interchangeably when referring to hard disks.) If the computer has more than one hard disk, or if the hard disk has been divided into multiple partitions, or *logical drives*, the additional drives are usually labeled D, E, F, and so on.

What Are Directories?

Because so much information can be stored on a disk, hard disks are usually divided into directories. For example, drive C typically has a separate directory for DOS (the Disk Operating System), a directory for Windows, and so on. Floppy disks can contain directories too, but usually don't. (Because of their limited capacity, it is easy to keep track of files on a floppy disk without using directories.)

Disk space is not set aside for individual directories; in fact, directories take up hardly any disk space at all. If you think of a disk as a file drawer full of papers, directories are like tabbed folders used to organize the papers into manageable groups.

What Are Files?

Directories hold files, just as folders hold pieces of paper. A file may contain the instructions for the computer to perform (typically called *program* or *executable files*). Or, a file may contain a text document that you can read (often referred to as a *document file*).

Regardless of the type of file, you can use Windows' File Manager to view and control them.

Starting the File Manager

To start the File Manager, follow these steps:

1. Open the Main group icon from the Program Manager window.

2. Open the File Manager program-item icon. The File
Manager appears.

Figure 12.1 shows the File Manager window. The
directory window's title bar shows the drive for the information displayed (in this case, drive C).

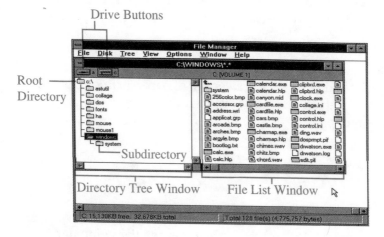

Figure 12.1 The File Manager window displaying
a directory window.

The Directory Tree

The left side of the directory window contains the directory
tree, a graphical representation of the directories and
subdirectories on your system. (The directory tree on your
screen will probably contain different directories from the
one shown in Figure 12.1.)

In Figure 12.1, you can see that the drive C contains a
directory called *windows*. The Windows directory has a

subdirectory: *system*. The right side of the window contains a list of the files in the directory currently highlighted on the directory tree. Notice that the folder icon next to the Windows directory (highlighted directory) appears as an open folder. In this example, the files in the Windows directory appear in the right half of the File manager window.

Changing Directories

When you change directories using the directory tree, it shows you the files in each directory. This is helpful if you are searching for a particular file to open, move, or copy.

To change the directory with the mouse, point to the directory you want and click. Table 12.1 shows which keys to use to change the directory with the keyboard.

Table 12.1 Keys to Change the Directory

Use This Key	To Change To
↑	The directory above the selected one.
↓	The directory below the selected one.
←	The subdirectory under the selected one.
→	The directory at higher level than the selected one.
Ctrl-↑	The previous directory at the same level.
Ctrl-↓	The next directory at the same level.
Home	The root directory.
End	The last directory in the tree.
First letter of name	Any specific directory.

The Root Directory The directory that leads to all other directories (much like the root of a tree leads to all branches and leaves) is the *root directory*. In Figure 12.1, the root directory is shown as C:\.

Subdirectories Any directory can have a subdirectory. You can think of it as having file folders within file folders; they help you organize your files. In Figure 12.1, *system* is a subdirectory of *windows*.

Notice that when you change to a new directory, the names of the files in the directory appear.

Expanding and Collapsing Directory Levels

As you noticed before, the directory tree shows the subdirectory of the Windows directory. You can *collapse* (decrease the detail of) the directory tree, so that the subdirectory does not appear. You can also *expand* (increase the detail of) the directory tree, so that subdirectories many levels deep will *all* show. Table 12.2 lists methods used to expand or collapse the directory levels.

Expand and Collapse Quickly Use the File Manager **Tree** menu to speed expanding and collapsing of multiple directories. Select Tree Expand Branch to expand all levels for the selected directory. Select Tree Expand All to expand the entire tree. Select Tree Collapse Branch to collapse the levels for the selected directory.

Table 12.2   Methods of Expanding or Collapsing
Directory Levels

Activity	Action
Expand with the mouse	Double-click on the directory icon.
Expand with the keyboard	Use the arrow keys to select the directory and press + (plus).
Collapse with the mouse	Double-click on the directory icon.
Collapse with the keyboard	Use the arrow keys to select the directory and press - (hyphen).

It's Only for Show   Collapsing and expanding
affects only this display; it doesn't alter your directories in any way.

Changing Drives

You can change drives to see the directories and files
contained on a different disk. To change drives with the
mouse, click on the drive icon in the upper left corner of the
Directory Tree window. To use the keyboard, press Ctrl-
drive letter (for example, press Ctrl-A for Drive A).

Can't Change Drives?   Make sure there is a disk
in the drive you are selecting. If there is not, a
warning message will appear instructing you to try
again.

Returning to the Program Manager

Each directory window can be minimized and maximized within File Manager, or closed altogether. If you have more than one directory window open at once, you may want to minimize all but the one you're working with.

You can also minimize or close the File Manager window itself to return to the Program Manager. If you're not going to use File Manager again right away, it is better to close it rather than minimize it, to conserve system resources.

To close the File Manager, double-click on the Control Menu box. Or, press Alt+F (for **F**ile), then X (for E**x**it).

In this lesson, you learned how to view the contents of drives and directories using the File Manager. In the next lesson, you'll learn how to create and delete directories with the File Manager.

Create or Delete a Directory with the File Manager

In this lesson, you will learn how to create and delete directories to organize your files.

Create a Directory

There are several reasons you may want to create a directory. Many application installation programs create a directory when you install the application on your computer. If one of your application installation programs does not, you will want to create a directory for the application.

A more common reason to create a directory is to store document files. For example, you may want to create a directory to store documents you create with Write. That way, the document files will not be scattered among the more than a hundred Windows program files in the Windows directory. Having a separate directory for Write documents can make it much easier to find and manipulate the documents you create.

To create a directory, follow these steps:

1. Open the File Manager. The directory window appears showing the directory tree and the files in the highlighted directory.

2. Highlight the directory under which you want the new directory to reside. (The directory you create will be a subdirectory of the directory you highlight.) If you don't want the new directory to be a subdirectory of another directory, highlight the root directory (C:\).

3. Choose File, Create Directory. The Create Directory dialog box appears.

4. Type the Name of the new directory, up to eight characters.

5. Select OK. The new directory is created.

Figure 13.1 illustrates the Create Directory dialog box for a new directory called WRITEDOC, a subdirectory of the Windows directory. Figure 13.2 shows the WRITEDOC directory added to the directory tree.

New Directory Name Text Box

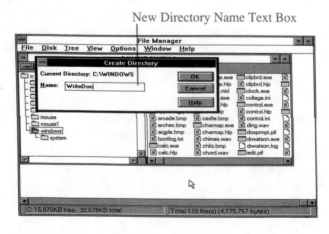

Figure 13.1 The Create Directory dialog box for the WRITEDOC directory.

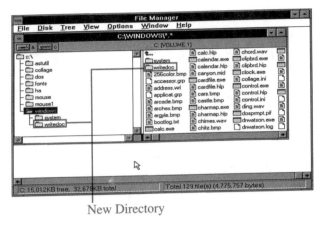

New Directory

Figure 13.2 The WRITEDOC directory is added.

Delete a Directory

You may need to delete a directory. For example, you may create a directory in the wrong spot on the directory tree. Or, you may want to remove the directory for an application you no longer use. You can delete a directory with the File Manager.

To delete a directory, follow these steps:

1. Make sure you have the necessary copies of any files in the directory you are going to delete. (The files must be deleted before the directory can be deleted.)

2. From the File Manager directory tree, highlight the directory you want to delete.

3. Choose File, Delete. The Delete dialog box appears.

4. Make sure the directory shown is correct. Select OK.

5. A Confirm Directory Delete dialog box appears. Check the directory again, then select OK.

6. If files are in the directory, a Confirm File Delete dialog box appears for each file. You must select OK to delete each file before the directory can be deleted.

Do I have to Confirm Every File?   The Delete Confirmation dialog box provides you a Yes to All command button to confirm the deletion of all files at once. Use this feature with caution.

I Hate When That Happens!   Be very careful any time you delete a directory. Make doubly certain you are deleting the correct directory.

In this lesson, you learned how to create and delete directories. In the next lesson, you will learn how to find specific files within directories.

Lesson 14

Find the File You Need with the File Manager

In this lesson, you will learn how to locate files quickly with the directory window and the Search command.

Opening and Closing a Directory Window

More than one directory window can be open at a time. This is useful when you are looking for files and even more useful when you want to copy or move files from one directory to another. (Copying and moving is covered in Lesson 15.)

To open a new directory window, choose Window, New Window from the File Manager. A window appears that is identical to the previous window except for the title on the window's title bar. Notice that each window's title now has a colon and a number following the name (see Figure 14.1). If you change the selected directory, the number disappears.

Shortcut to Creating a New Directory Window If you want the new window to display the contents of another disk drive, simply double click on that drive's icon. Single-clicking the icon displays the drive's contents in the current window, double-clicking opens a new window to display the contents of the drive.

Window #1

Window #2

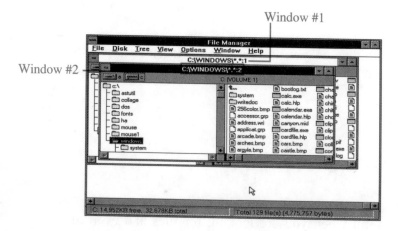

Figure 14.1 When a second window is opened, File Manager attaches a colon and a number (:1, :2) to each window title.

Arranging Windows Remember, you can arrange your windows using **Window, Cascade** or **Window, Tile.** The **Window** menu also lists the windows, placing a check mark in front of the active window.

When you're finished with a directory window, close it by double-clicking on the Control Menu box or pressing Ctrl-F4.

Changing the Display

The File Manager's View menu controls how the directory window displays information.

In the examples you've seen, the directory tree and the list of files were both shown. You can choose to show only one or the other, and you can change the way each is shown.

To show only the tree, choose View, Tree Only; to show only the list of files (the *directory*), choose View, Directory Only. To show them both again, choose View, Tree and Directory.

If you elect to display both the tree and directory, you can change the amount of window space allotted to each. For example, you may want to see more files and less white space around the tree. Follow these steps to change the way the window space is divided between the panes.

1. Choose View, Split. A black line appears in the directory window, representing the divider between the two panes.

2. Use the mouse pointer or arrow keys to move the black line to the desired location (as shown in Figure 14.2).

3. Press Enter when the line is where you want it. The window display is changed (see Figure 14.3).

In Figure 14.3, only file names and icons are shown in the directory. The File Manager can display more information about each file if you desire. Choose View, All File Details to display the following information about each file:

- Size in bytes

- Last modification date

- Last modification time

- File attributes (to identify whether a file is hidden, system, archive, or read only)

Or, choose View, Partial Details to identify which of the above information you want displayed.

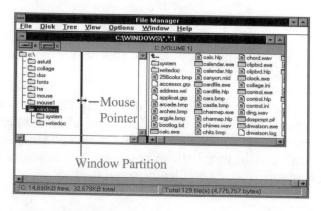

Figure 14.2 The line to select the split.

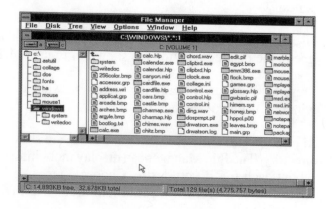

Figure 14.3 The completed split.

Controlling the Order of the Display

As shown in Figure 14.3, the files in the directory are in alphabetical order by file name. You may also sort the directory display by the following methods:

- **V**iew, Sort **b**y Type arranges files alphabetically by extension. For example, *sample.doc* would come before *file.txt*, which would come before *budget.wri*.

- **V**iew, Sort by **S**ize arranges files by size from largest to smallest.

- **V**iew, Sort by **D**ate arranges files by date from newest to oldest.

- **V**iew, By File **T**ype opens a dialog box that allows you to select certain types of files to include or exclude in the listing (program files, document files, directories, and so on).

After experimenting with these arrangements, you can restore the default setting by choosing View, Sort by Name.

Updating a Directory Window

Most often, when you create, change, or delete a file, the directory window is updated immediately. If it is not (as is the case with some networks), you can update the directory window yourself. Simply choose Window, Refresh (F5 is the keyboard shortcut to refreshing a window).

If you add or delete directories from the DOS prompt (either outside of Windows or from Windows' DOS shell), it may be necessary to use **W**indow, **R**efresh to get File Manager to "see" a directory or file that you created from the DOS prompt, or to realize that one you deleted using DOS is gone.

Searching for a File

As you create more files, the ability to find a specific file becomes more critical. You can search for either a single file or a group of files with similar names using the **F**ile, **S**earch command. To search for a group of files, use the wildcard * (asterisk) with a partial file name to narrow down the search. Table 14.1 shows some search examples and their potential results.

Table 14.1   Search Results Examples

Characters Entered For Search	Sample Search Results
`rpt1.wri`	rpt1.wri
`rpt*.wri`	rpt1.wri, rpt2.wri, rpt11.wri
`c*.exe`	calc.exe, calendar.exe
`*.exe`	calc.exe, calendar.exe, notepad.exe
`c*.*`	calc.exe, calendar.exe, class.wri

To search for a file, follow these steps:

1. From the File Manager, choose **F**ile, **S**earch. The Search dialog box appears (see Figure 14.4).

2. In the Search For text area, enter the characters to search for. Use wildcards to identify unknown characters.

3. If you would like to search the entire drive, type c:\ in the Start From text box and make sure the Search All Subdirectories check box is active.

If you would like to search only a certain directory and its subdirectories, type it in the Start From text box.

To search a single directory (no subdirectories), type it in the Start From text box and make sure the Search All Subdirectories check box is not active.

4. Select OK to begin the search. The Search Results window appears, showing the files that were found (see Figure 14.5).

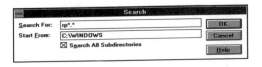

Figure 14.4   The completed Search dialog box.

Figure 14.5   The search results.

In this lesson, you learned how to open and close directory windows, change the display and the order of the files shown, and update a directory window. You also learned how to search for a file through one or more directories. In the next lesson, you will learn how to move, copy, rename, and delete files and directories.

89

Managing Files and Directories with the File Manager

In this lesson, you will learn how to move, copy, rename, and delete files and directories.

Selecting and Deselecting Files or Directories

Before you can move, copy, rename, or delete files or directories, you must identify, or *select,* the ones you want. The following sections tell you how.

Select a Single File or Directory

To select a single file or directory from the File Manager's directory window, click on it. Or, press Tab to move the highlight bar from the directory tree to the directory window, and then use the keys shown in Table 15.1.

Selecting Multiple Contiguous Files or Directories

Selecting a single file is useful, but to really speed up operations, you will want to select multiple files and then execute commands that will affect the entire group. For example, you may want to select several files to be copied to a disk. Copying them all at once is much faster than copying each file individually.

Table 15.1   Keys to Select a File or Directory

Use This Key	To Select
↑	Previous file or directory
↓	Next file or directory
→	Subdirectory or file to the right
←	Higher level directory or file to the left
Home	First file or directory
End	Last file or directory
First letter of the name	Next file or directory starting with a given letter

It is easy to select multiple files or directories that are displayed contiguously in the File Manager directory window. Figure 15.1 illustrates a selection of contiguous files.

Contiguous Files   When the files that you want to select are listed together in the File Manager, without any files that you *don't* want between them, they are *contiguous*.

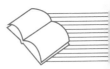

To select contiguous files or directories with the mouse:

1. Click on the first file or directory that you want to select. When you click on it, it is highlighted.

2. Hold down the Shift key and click on the last file or directory that you want to select. All the items between the first and last selections are highlighted (including the first and last selections themselves).

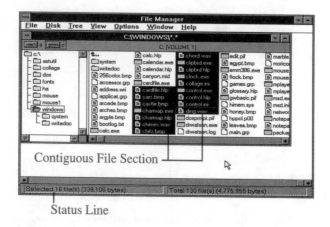

Figure 15.1 Selecting contiguous files.

To select contiguous files or directories with the keyboard:

1. Use the arrow keys to move the highlight to the first file or directory that you want to select. (Press Tab to move the highlight bar between the directory tree and the directory window.)

2. Hold down the Shift key and use the arrow keys to extend the highlight to the last file or directory you want to select.

To deselect a contiguous group of files or directories, select a file or directory outside the selected items.

Selecting Noncontiguous Files or Directories

Often, the files or directories you want to select are not contiguous but separated by several files that you do not want. However, this is not a problem. You can use the Ctrl key to select them.

To select or deselect an item with the mouse, hold down the Ctrl key while you click on the file or directory. The item you click on will be highlighted, and any other items you click on (while holding down the Ctrl key) will remain highlighted too.

With the keyboard it's a little more work, but still easy. Select or deselect individual items with the keyboard using the following steps:

1. Use the arrow keys to highlight the first file or directory that you want to select.

2. Press and release Shift-F8. The file or directory is highlighted and the line around the selection blinks.

3. Move the highlight bar to the next item you want to select, and press the space bar. That file or directory is highlighted too.

4. Continue to select (or deselect) files or directories. When you are done, press Shift-F8 again.

Narrowing the Selection   If you want to select or deselect files with related names, choose the File, Select Files command. Enter the file name in the Select Files dialog box. Then, choose Select or Deselect. For example, you may want to select all Write document files with a .WRI extension, then deselect a few of the files individually if you don't want them all for your activity.

93

Figure 15.2 shows multiple noncontiguous files selected.

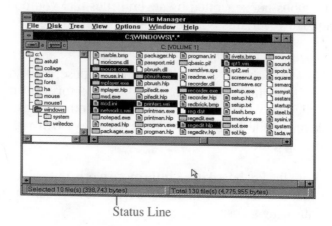

Status Line

Figure 15.2   Selecting multiple noncontiguous files.

Moving or Copying Files or Directories

To move or copy files or directories through the File Manager, you *drag and drop*—that is, you select the items you want from your *source* directory, "drag" them to the *destination* directory, and then "drop" them there. You'll learn this technique in more detail in the steps that follow.

Move vs. Copy   *Move* means the file or directory is no longer in the original spot but is in the new location. *Copy* means the original file or directory remains in the original spot, and a new copy of the file or directory is in a second location.

Before you move or copy, make sure the source directory window is visible, so you can highlight the file(s) that you're going to drag. Also, make sure that the destination drive or directory is visible, either as an open window or as an icon.

If you're copying between two directories, you can open both directory windows and then choose Window, Tile. Figure 15.3 shows a tiled display of the WINDOWS directory window (the *source* directory), and the empty WRITEDOC directory (the *destination* directory) ready for file copying.

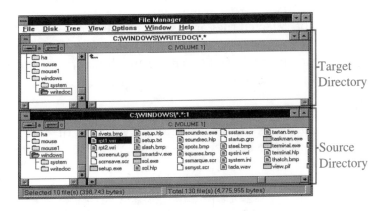

Figure 15.3 Two windows ready for moving or copying files.

Copying Files and Directories

With the mouse, use this procedure to copy:

1. Select the files or directories to copy.

2. Press the Ctrl key and drag the files or directories to the destination drive, window, or icon.

3. Release the mouse button and the Ctrl key.

4. A dialog box appears asking you to confirm the copy. Click on OK.

With the keyboard, use this procedure to copy:

1. Select the files or directories to copy.

2. Choose File, Copy. The Copy dialog box appears.

3. The selected files are listed in the From text box. Type the desired destination in the To text box, including the path to the destination drive and directory. Figure 15.4 shows a completed Copy dialog box.

4. Select OK by pressing the Enter key. Figure 15.5 illustrates the result of the copy. The Write document files have been copied into the WriteDoc directory.

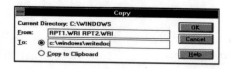

Figure 15.4 The Copy dialog box completed.

The File Is Already There If you attempt to copy a file or directory to a location where an identical file or directory exists, Windows lets you know with a message.

96

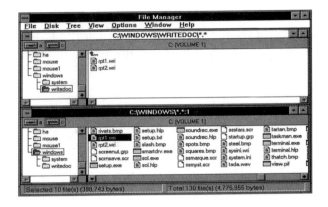

Figure 15.5 The completed copy operation.

Moving Files and Directories

With the mouse, use these steps to complete a move:

1. Select the files or directories to move.

2. Drag the files or directories to the drive, window, or icon.

3. Release the mouse button.

4. A dialog box appears asking you to confirm the move. Click on OK.

With the keyboard, complete a move using these steps:

1. Select the files or directories to move.

2. Choose File, Move. The Move dialog box appears.

3. The selected files or directories are listed in the **From** text box. Type the desired destination in the **To** text box, including the path to the destination drive and directory.

4. Select OK by pressing the Enter key.

Renaming Files or Directories

To rename your files, follow these steps:

1. Select the file or directory to rename.

2. Choose File, Rename. The Rename dialog box appears.

3. In the **To** text box, type in the new name for the file or directory.

4. Select OK.

 It Worked Yesterday Don't rename program files. Many applications will not work if their files have been renamed.

Deleting Files or Directories

You can delete files or directories, but be careful. Before you delete anything, it is a good idea to make a backup copy of any files or directories you might need later.

Better Safe than Sorry   A common use for the delete command is to delete the original after a file has been copied. Moving the file would accomplish the same result, but it's safer to copy, because you still have the original in case anything goes wrong.

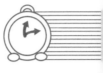

To delete, follow these steps:

1. Select the file or directory to delete.

2. Choose File, Delete. The Delete dialog box appears, indicating what will be deleted.

3. Check the Delete dialog box carefully to make certain you are deleting what you intended to delete.

4. Select OK. You will be asked to confirm the deletion. If you are deleting a directory and there are files which must be deleted first, you will be asked to confirm each file deletion.

In this lesson, you learned how to copy, move, rename, and delete files and directories. In the next lesson, you will continue to enhance your skills with the File Manager by using it to format and copy floppy disks.

Formatting and Copying Floppy Disks with the File Manager

In this lesson, you will learn how to format and copy a floppy disk using the File Manager.

Formatting a Floppy Disk

When you buy a box of floppy disks, the floppy disks are usually unformatted. (You can buy formatted disks, but they're more expensive.) They're sold unformatted because some computers use operating systems other than DOS, and such systems need to format the floppy disks in their own format.

Therefore, before you can use a new floppy disk, you must format it to work with your computer's operating system (DOS). Formatting prepares the floppy disk by organizing its space into *sectors* and creating a *file allocation table* (*FAT*) to keep track of the data stored in each sector.

Recycled Disks You can format and reformat a floppy disk as often as you wish. When you format a previously used floppy disk, any files that were on the floppy disk are lost. Before formatting a used floppy disk, be certain the floppy disk does not contain files you want to keep.

Disks can be formatted from the DOS command line, but you may find it more convenient to format disks from within the File Manager. Follow these steps to format a floppy disk:

1. Insert the floppy disk into the drive.

2. From the File Manager, choose Disk, Format Disk. The Format Disk dialog box appears (see Figure 16.1).

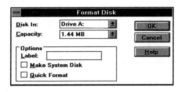

Figure 16.1   The Format Disk dialog box.

3. From the Format Disk dialog box, use the Disk In: drop-down list to select the drive the floppy disk is in.

4. Use the drop-down list to select the Capacity. Refer to Table 16.1 for a list of capacity choices.

5. Select OK.

6. A confirmation box appears. Carefully check the information.

7. Once you are certain the information for formatting is correct, select OK. The disk drive lights up during formatting and a message appears on your screen identifying how much of the formatting process is complete.

8. When the process is over, the Format Complete dialog box appears, listing the amount of space available on

the newly formatted floppy disk and asking if you want to format another floppy disk. Select Yes to format another, or No to stop formatting.

Table 16.1 Floppy Disk Capacity to Specify when Formatting

Disk Diameter	Disk Density	Capacities Available
3.5"	Double	720KB
3.5"	High	1.44MB
5.25"	Double	360KB
5.25"	High	360KB or 1.2MB

High-density 5.25" floppy disks can be formatted at either 360KB or 1.2MB capacity, but high-density 3.5" floppy disks can be formatted at only one capacity: 1.44MB.

Your Floppy Disk Won't Format If the floppy disk has errors that prevent it from being formatted, Windows will tell you. Throw out any floppy disks that cannot be formatted or have problems during the formatting process. If the floppy disk is a high-density 3.5" floppy disk, make sure you format it at 1.44MB capacity; if you try to format a high-density 3.5" floppy disk at 720KB capacity, Windows will (falsely) report that the floppy disk has errors.

It is always a good idea to keep several formatted floppy disks available in case you need to move or copy files in a hurry.

Making System Disks

What Is a System Disk?   A system disk contains operating system files you need to start your computer in the event your hard disk fails. With it, you can start your computer from the floppy disk drive.

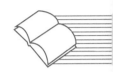

You should always have at least one system disk on hand in case something goes wrong. A hard disk problem can lock you out of your system unless you have a system disk—so can an error in your CONFIG.SYS or AUTOEXEC.BAT file. With a system disk, you can boot from the floppy drive, bypassing the hard drive (*and* the error) until the problem can be found and corrected.

More than One Drive   If you have two floppy disk drives (A and B) of differing sizes (5.25" and 3.5"), your system disk must be the kind that fits on drive A (usually the 5.25" one). This is because when your computer boots, it checks drive A first for a disk, and if it finds none, it boots from the hard disk. It never checks drive B when booting, so you can't boot from there.

You can create a system disk when you format the floppy disk by checking the Make System Disk check box in the Format Disk dialog box. Or, to make a formatted floppy disk into a system disk, follow these steps:

1. From the File Manager directory window, select the icon for your hard disk. (This is where the operating system files reside.)

2. Insert a formatted floppy disk into drive A.

3. Choose Disk, Make System Disk. The Make System Disk dialog box appears for you to verify the drive.

4. Once you have verified the drive, select Yes. A message appears telling you that the system disk is being created. When the message disappears, the system disk is created.

Create a system disk for your computer and store it in a safe place. Someday you'll be glad that you took this precaution.

Copying a Floppy Disk

Disk Duplicating Made Easy Even if you are accustomed to doing your file and disk operations from the DOS prompt (moving, copying, formatting, deleting, and so forth), you might want to use the File Manager for copying disks, because unlike DOS, the File Manager does not require you to swap disks repeatedly when copying disks with higher capacities than 360KB.

If you want to copy *all* the files on one floppy disk to another, rather than each one individually, you can do it easily with the File Manager. The only condition is that both floppy disks must be of the same capacity. For example, if the source floppy disk is 1.44MB (high density), the destination floppy disk must also be 1.44MB.

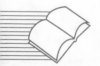

Which Is Which? The *source* floppy disk is the one you are copying from. The *destination* floppy disk is the one you are copying to.

Proceed with Caution   When you copy a floppy disk, all files previously on the destination floppy disk are lost.

Follow these steps to copy a floppy disk:

1. Place the source floppy disk in the drive to copy *from.* If you have two drives of the same size and capacity, place the destination floppy disk in the drive to copy *to.*

2. From the File Manager, select the drive of the source floppy disk.

3. Choose Disk, Copy Disk.

4. A message appears reminding you that all the files on the destination floppy disk will be erased. Select Yes to go on.

5. The Copy Disk dialog box appears. If you are using two drives, the floppy disk will be copied without your having to swap floppy disks. If you are using one drive, Windows will instruct you when to swap the source and destination floppy disks. Follow the instructions.

In this lesson, you learned how to format disks and how to copy an entire floppy disk. You also learned how to create a system disk. The next lesson will conclude your work with the File Manager. You will learn how to start an application from the File Manager.

Starting an Application from the File Manager

In this lesson, you will learn how to start an application from within the File Manager.

Using the Run Command

In Lesson 7, you learned how to start an application using the application icon or the **File**, **Run** command from the Program Manager window. You can't select application icons from the File Manager, but you can still use the **File**, **Run** command.

There are several advantages of using the **Run** command from the File Manager:

- You can sort the files using **View**, **Sort by Type**, which lets you see all the *executable* (*.EXE*) files grouped together. This allows you to quickly find the file that starts the program you want to use.

- No typing is required to start the application. You select the directory from the directory tree and the file from the directory window. Then, when you use the **File**, **Run** command, all the information is already entered in

the appropriate blanks. Figure 17.1 shows the Run
dialog box with the .EXE file for the Solitaire game
ready to be run.

• You can specify start-up parameters for the application,
  just as you can from the DOS command line. (The manual
  for the application describes different start-up options.)

Figure 17.1   The Run dialog box with the Solitaire
game .EXE file ready to run.

To use the **F**ile, **R**un command, follow these steps:

1. To reduce typing, select the appropriate directory and
   executable file from the File Manager directory tree and
   window.

2. From the File Manager window, choose File, Run. The
   Run dialog box appears.

3. When the command and any start-up options are entered, select OK.

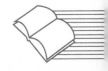

Executable Files   Applications are started from
executable files. These typically end in .EXE. Some
applications are started from executable files that
end in .COM, or from batch files (which end in
.BAT), but this is less common.

Selecting the File to Run

There are other ways to start an application from the File Manager. You can locate the executable file and double-click on it. More importantly, Windows 3.1 allows you to open an application by double-clicking on a document created by the application.

Starting an Application from the Executable File

You can double-click on an executable file to start the application, rather than using the File, Run command. Note that you cannot add start-up parameters to the command. The advantage is that you can start an application from the directory window and bypass the Run command dialog box.

Starting an Application from an Associated File

There are three common types of file icons displayed by the File Manager. The one that looks like a miniature window indicates that this file is an executable file. This icon will appear next to all .EXE, .COM, and .BAT files.

The other icons (which look like pieces of paper with a corner turned down) indicate that the file is a document file. Some of these icons are blank and some have lines on them. The lines indicate that Windows knows what application created the document file. If you double-click on one of these icons, the *associated application* will open with the file you chose in a document window.

File association is a very powerful feature of Windows 3.1. It allows you to drag a document icon to different applications for processing. For instance, you can print an associated file simply by dragging its icon from the File Manager and dropping it into the Print Manager icon. This allows you to print a document (for example, a Write document) without having to open the application first.

Using Drag and Drop to Create Program-Item Icons

In Lesson 11, you learned how to add program-item icons to Program Manager groups. You can also add program-item icons to Program Manager groups using the File Manager. This procedure will likely test your ability to work with multiple open windows, but once you get the hang of it, you'll be on your way to becoming a Windows "power user."

To create a new program-item icon using the File Manager, follow these steps:

1. Open the File Manager and locate the executable file that you want to appear as a program-item icon in a Program Manager group.

Give yourself room to work You know that you will have to be able to see both the Program Manager window and the File Manager window to be able to complete this task. When you start the File Manager, resize the window to allow room on screen for the Program Manager window (see Figure 17.2).

2. Switch Tasks back to the Program Manager. Resize the Program Manager window so that you are able to see both the File Manager window and Program Manager window (see Figure 17.2). You should also be able to see the group icon or window to which you wish to add the program-item icon.

To view all your groups in one window The easiest way to see all your groups (especially in a small Program Manager window) is to iconize (minimize from a window to an icon) all the groups. Once all your groups are iconized, choose Window, Arrange Icons to bring all the group icons into view.

3. Drag the file in question from the File Manager to the Program Manager group to which you want to add the program-item icon.

4. When the mouse pointer is positioned over the appropriate Program Manager group window or icon, drop (release the mouse button) the file into the group. A new program-item icon appears in the group.

Notice that as you drag the file between the File Manager and the Program Manager, the mouse pointer appears as a circle with a line through it (like a no smoking sign). This indicates that you cannot drop the file where the pointer is located (if you do, nothing will happen). When the mouse pointer is positioned over a Program Manager group window or icon, it turns into the familiar arrow pointer and a document icon with a plus sign in it (see Figure 17.2). This indicates that you can drop the file here.

As you can see, you can drag and drop executable files into a Program Manager group and they become program-item icons. Windows 3.1 allows you to do this with associated document files as well. For example, if you have a document that you work with regularly (i.e., Journal of Customer Service Calls), you can drag it to the Program Manager and drop it into a group. The new program-item will take the icon of the associated application. You can double-click the icon to open the application and the document at the same time.

File Manager Window   Program Manager Window

Executive
File Icon

Document
Icon

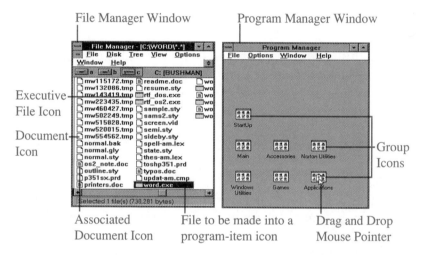

Group
Icons

Associated
Document Icon

File to be made into a
program-item icon

Drag and Drop
Mouse Pointer

Figure 17.2   Dragging a file from the File Manager to a Program Manager group.

Lesson 18
Getting Ready to Print

In this lesson, you will learn how to get ready to print, and how to set up any special typefaces.

Checking the Printer Installation

When you installed Windows, you configured the printer and the link to the printer. This is important because almost all Windows applications print using the Print Manager and the default printer defined through it. Before you attempt to print, you need to check Windows to make sure the settings are correct.

To check the print setup from Windows, go to the Printers dialog box using the following steps:

1. From the Program Manager, open the Main group icon.

2. Open the Control Panel program-item icon from the Main group window.

3. Open the Printers icon. The Printers dialog box appears (see Figure 18.1).

To Setup Printers

Default Printer

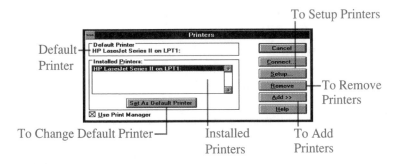

To Remove Printers

To Change Default Printer

Installed Printers

To Add Printers

Figure 18.1   The Printers dialog box.

Default vs. Installed Printer   The Printers dialog box identifies the Default Printer and the Installed Printers. The Default Printer is the one that the computer assumes is connected to your computer unless you select another printer. The Installed Printers are those for which special instructions (called *Printer Drivers*) are available on your computer. You can select an Installed Printer and then select the Set As Default Printer button to make it the Default Printer.

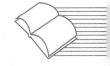

From the Printers dialog box, you can select the following buttons to check the settings.

- The Connect button opens the Connect dialog box. On it, you can see the port (connection) to which your printer is attached. This port is usually LPT1 (for parallel printers) or COM1 (for serial printers).

  The Connect dialog box allows you to check or change the settings which control the timeout periods for the Print Manager. Timeouts define the length of time the Print Manager will wait to inform you of a printing problem.

113

Printer Port The printer port is the connection on your computer to which the cable to your printer is attached. If the port description indicates Not Present, this means Windows does not detect that port on your computer. Check your printer manual to see whether your printer is parallel or serial and, therefore, will use the parallel or serial port.

- The Setup button allows you to enter information about your printer setup (see the dialog box in Figure 18.2). You can define the following:

  The **R**esolution in dots per inch (the more dots the finer the resolution).

  The Paper Size, the Paper Source.

  The amount of **M**emory in your printer (check your printer manual if you are not sure).

  The Orientation to either **P**ortrait (the short side of the paper is at the top) or **L**andscape (the long side of paper is at the top).

  The number of Copies to print.

- The **A**dd button lets you add new printers to the Installed **P**rinters list. Just select the name of the printer, and then select the Install button.

What disk? When you install new features to your Windows environment, have your installation diskettes close at hand. In the example above, Windows will probably ask you to insert one of the disks containing the printer drivers before it can carry out your instructions.

Type of Printer Being Set Up

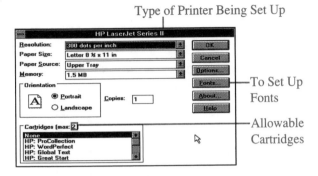

To Set Up
Fonts

Allowable
Cartridges

Figure 18.2   The dialog box for setting up your
printer.

Once you have all the setup options in place, you may
return to the Control Panel.

In addition to making sure Windows is ready for printing, you'll want to check your equipment. Things to double-
check include:

- Is the cable between the computer and the printer
  securely attached on each end?

- Is the printer turned on?

- Is the printer ready for the computer's transmission
  with the ON LINE light on?

- Is paper loaded in the printer?

Working with Fonts

Many printers can print more than one character style or
typeface (called a *font*). Check your printer manual to see if

115

it is capable of printing multiple fonts. If it is, you will want to check the font setup in Windows before printing.

Where Are These Fonts? Fonts may be stored on disks or on cartridges which slide into the printer.

When you set up Windows, the fonts for your printer were identified. The dialog box shown in Figure 18.3 refers to an HP LaserJet Series II printer. Cartridges are commonly sold for this printer. The cartridge B:Times Proportional 1 has been selected. A maximum of two cartridges may be selected for this printer at one time.

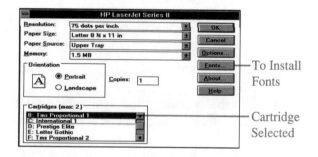

Figure 18.3 Font cartridge selected.

Use the Fonts button on the dialog box shown in Figure 18.3 to open the Font Installer dialog box. You can determine which fonts are installed from this dialog box.

To check the font setup:

1. From the Program Manager Main group window, open the Control Panel.

2. Open the Printers icon.

3. Select Setup on the Printers dialog box.

4. If your fonts are stored on cartridges, highlight the cartridge(s) you will use (based on the maximum number identified in the dialog box).

5. If your fonts are stored on floppy disk, select the Fonts button. The Font Installer dialog box appears. You may select the font you want from the list of available fonts.

Installing TrueType Fonts

Windows 3.1 comes with a number of TrueType fonts. These are fonts that appear in your printed document exactly as they do on your screen. The information your printer needs to print TrueType fonts is downloaded to your printer each time you print a document containing them.

Figure 18.4 shows the Fonts Installer dialog box with a number of TrueType fonts installed. To add fonts, follow these steps:

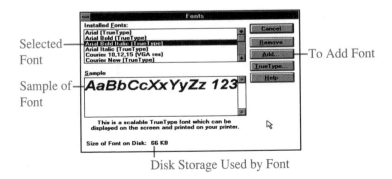

Figure 18.4   The Fonts dialog box.

1. From the Program Manager, open the Control Panel.

2. Open the Fonts icon. The Fonts dialog box, shown in Figure 18.4, appears.

3. Select Add from the Fonts dialog box.

4. From the Add Font File dialog box, select the directory where the font file is located, select the font to add, and select OK.

5. Once the font is added, you may add another font or close the dialog box.

Removing a Font from Memory or Disk

Fonts take up space in active memory as well as your hard disk. You may want to delete fonts you do not use to free memory or remove them entirely from your disk. To remove fonts, follow these steps:

1. From the Program Manager, open the Control Panel.

2. Open the Fonts icon. The Fonts dialog box appears.

3. Select the font to remove, and then select the Remove button.

4. A message appears for you to verify the removal. If you leave the Delete Font File from Disk box unchecked, the font is only removed from active memory. Check the box and the font file is removed from the hard disk as well.

In this lesson, you learned how to prepare to print. In the next lesson, you will learn how to print with the Print Manager.

Lesson 19

Printing with the Print Manager

In this lesson, you will learn how to print through the Print Manager and check the status of your print jobs.

Purpose of the Print Manager

The Print Manager acts as the "middleman" between your printer and the application you are printing from. When you choose **File**, **Print** from most Windows applications, the font and file information is handed off to the Print Manager. The Print Manager then feeds the information to the printer. This allows you to continue working in your application while your job is printed.

Print Jobs A *print job* (or simply *job*) is created when you choose the Print command from the application in which you are working.

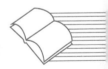

Checking the Print Queue

When you print a document, the printer usually begins processing the job immediately. What happens if the printer is working on another job, sent by you or, in the case of a network printer, someone else? In this case, the Print Manager acts as a print queue and holds the job until the printer is ready for it.

 Print Queue The *print queue* is a holding area for jobs that have to be printed. If you were to list the contents of the queue, the jobs would appear in the order they were sent to the Print Manager.

Figure 19.1 illustrates the document NETWORKS.WRI in the print queue. As you can see, the percent of the document which has been printed is shown (34% of 63KB) along with the time and date the document was sent to print. Notice also that the printer is shown to be printing. This indicates the document was just sent to the queue and is beginning to print.

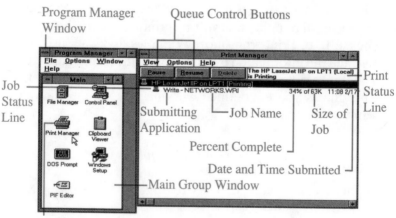

Figure 19.1   The Print Manager print queue window.

To display the print queue, follow these steps:

1. From the Program Manager, open the Main group icon.

2. Open the Print Manager icon (see Figure 19.1).

3. The Print Manager window appears with a list of *queued* documents. If no documents are waiting to print, a message tells you the printer is idle.

Controlling the Print Job

You can control print jobs once they are in the queue. This includes changing the order in which the jobs print, pausing and resuming the print job, or deleting a job before it prints.

Reordering Jobs in the Queue

To use the mouse to change the order of a job in the queue, drag the job entry to a new position in the list. To use the keyboard to reposition a job in the queue:

1. From the Print Manager window, use the arrow keys to highlight the document to be repositioned.

2. Hold down Ctrl and use the arrow keys to move the job to the new position in the queue.

3. Release the Ctrl key.

First Come, First Served   You cannot reorder or place a job before the job that is currently printing.

Pausing and Resuming the Print Queue

You may want to pause the queue and then resume printing later. For example, the paper in the printer may be misaligned. Pausing the print queue will give you time to correct the problem.

To pause the print queue, select the Pause button or press Alt-P while in the Print Manager window. To resume printing, select the Resume button or press Alt-R.

Printer Stalled   Your printer may stall while it is processing your print job. If it does, stalled will appear in the printer status line. Press Alt-R to start printing again. Chances are that a problem somewhere along the line caused the printer to stall, the queue will stall again, and you will have to solve the problem.

Delete a Print Job

Sometimes, you'll send a document to be printed and then change your mind. For example, you may think of other text to add to the document or realize you forgot to spell-check your work. In such a case, deleting the print job is easy. Follow these steps:

1. From the Print Manager window, select the job to delete.

2. Select the Delete button or press Alt-D.

3. A message appears for you to confirm the deletion.

4. Select OK.

Clear the Queue! To delete all the files in the print queue, choose View, Exit from the Print Manager menu bar or double-click the Control Menu box. Select OK from the Print Manager dialog box.

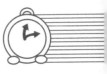

Controlling Windows Appearance with the Control Panel

In this lesson, you will learn how to change the look and performance of Windows by using the Control Panel.

The Control Panel is an application in the Main group that allows you to control many aspects of Windows (see Figure 20.1). Those discussed in this lesson include:

- Colors displayed on-screen.

- What appears on your desktop.

- International language and display support.

Control the Color of Window Elements

Control Panel

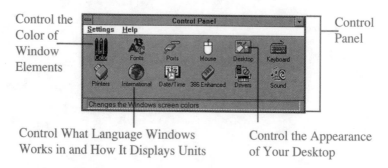

Control What Language Windows Works in and How It Displays Units

Control the Appearance of Your Desktop

Figure 20.1   The Windows Control Panel.

Setting Colors

You can change the color of many components of Windows with the Control Panel. This can be important if you have a monochrome or LCD screen. These screens may not have the ability to display certain colors. This could cause a real problem if the color chosen to display command buttons can not be displayed by your screen. Windows comes with several predefined color schemes for users with monochrome or LCD screens. The ability to control the color of certain Windows' elements can also help you learn to use Windows faster. This is because you are able to look for a particular color and shape, instead of just a shape. Finally, you can adjust the colors displayed on your color monitor just for a change of pace.

Change colors with these steps:

1. From the Program Manager, open the Main group icon and then open the Control Panel.

2. Open the Color program-item. The Color dialog box appears.

3. Open the Schemes drop-down list box by clicking on the down arrow button or pressing Alt-↓. The predefined options appear (see Figure 20.2).

4. Use the arrow keys to scroll through the color scheme options. The display below Color Schemes illustrates the current selection.

5. Press Enter to select your choice.

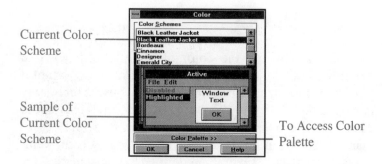

Current Color Scheme

Sample of Current Color Scheme

To Access Color Palette

Figure 20.2 The Black Leather Jacket Color Scheme selected on the Color dialog box.

Test Your Artistic Aptitude After you become more comfortable with Windows, go into the Color dialog box and create your own color scheme. Select the Show Palette button. A new section of the Color dialog box appears. This will allow you to assign different colors to the various Windows components (title bar, buttons, menus, and so on). You can then save your creation as a Windows color scheme.

Changing the Desktop

Many visual and performance elements of your desktop can be changed through the Control Panel. The Desktop dialog box shown in Figure 20.3 has the following options.

Pattern Name Select the pattern that is displayed on the desktop. This is a simple, two-color pattern (defined in the Color dialog box).

Applications Identify the speed at which windows cycle when you press Alt-Tab. This is the fast task-switching that Windows 3.1 offers.

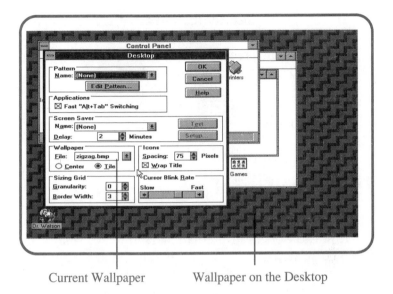

Current Wallpaper   Wallpaper on the Desktop

Figure 20.3 Desktop dialog box with Zigzag Wallpaper selected.

Screen Saver If the same image remains on your screen for an extended period of time, you could damage your monitor. By selecting a screen saver, when your computer is inactive for the default time, Windows will automatically blank the screen and run a pattern across your screen. To continue working, press a key or move the mouse.

Wallpaper More elaborate than the Pattern selection, the Wallpaper option allows you to display .BMP files on your desktop. Windows comes with some very attractive wallpapers, or you can use Paintbrush to create your own.

Icons Determine icon Spacing and whether icon titles are wrapped to another line or cut off.

Sizing Grid   Identify the setting of the "magnetic" grid which aligns windows and icons. **G**ranularity determines the precision of the grid, and **B**order Width sets the size of the border of windows.

Cursor Blink Rate   Set how fast the cursor (your marker in text boxes) blinks.

Habla Usted Espanol?

Most readers will be using Windows in the United States. But if you do work in an international setting, you may want to make some changes on the International dialog box. Figure 20.4 shows the dialog box with these settings:

- **C**ountry—Windows has a number of standard country settings on how units are displayed, page setup defaults, etc. Use this option to choose the Country's settings you wish to use.

- **L**anguage—Some Windows' applications provide foreign language support. Use this option to choose which language you want to work with.

- **K**eyboard Layout—Windows supports a number of keyboard layouts. This controls the way keys are mapped to the special characters associated with the **L**anguage you have chosen to work with.

- **M**easurement—Use this drop-down list to choose which measurement system you want to work with, English or Metric.

- **L**ist Separator—In this text box, enter the character with which you want to separate elements of a list.

- **D**ate Format—Use this command button to change the way long and short dates are displayed.

- Currency Format—Use this command button to change the way positive and negative currency values are displayed.

- **T**ime Format—Use this command button to change the way time values are displayed.

- **N**umber Format—Use this command button to change the way numbers are displayed.

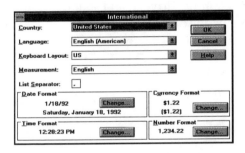

Figure 20.4   The International dialog box.

To control the international settings, follow these steps:

1. From the Control Panel window, open the International icon. The International dialog box appears.

2. Make the selections for the changes you desire.

3. Select OK. The changes take effect.

In this lesson, you learned how to set colors, change the desktop appearance, and give Windows an international flavor. In the next lesson, you will learn to use the Control Panel to control hardware settings.

129

Controlling Hardware Settings with the Control Panel

In this lesson, you will learn to use the Control Panel to control hardware settings for ports, mouse, keyboard, date/time, drivers, and sound. Figure 21.1 displays the Control Panel and points out the icons you will be using in this lesson.

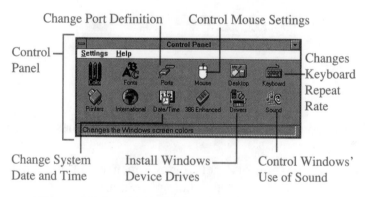

Change Port Definition · Control Mouse Settings

Control Panel

Changes Keyboard Repeat Rate

Change System Date and Time · Install Windows Device Drives · Control Windows' Use of Sound

Figure 21.1 The Windows Control Panel.

Altering the Date and Time

The system date and time is set in your computer. This is used to time-stamp files as they are created or modified.

Also, many application programs allow you to automatically insert the date and time on-screen or when you print. Always make sure the date and time are correct.

To check or set the date and time, follow these steps:

1. From the Control Panel, open the Date/Time icon. The Date & Time dialog box appears (see Figure 21.2).

2. Use the Tab key or the mouse to move between digits in the date and time. Enter the appropriate date and time. To use the mouse, click on the portion of the date or time you want to change and click on the up or down arrow button to increment or decrement the value accordingly.

3. Select OK or press Enter to accept the changes you have made. Press Esc or select Cancel to close the dialog box without saving changes.

Figure 21.2   The Date & Time dialog box.

Modifying Mouse Settings

You can modify the settings for your mouse. The following settings can be changed:

- The speed of mouse tracking (how fast/far the pointer moves when you move the mouse).

131

- The speed of the double-click *(the time allowed between the first and second click so that your action is recognized as a double-click and not just two single-clicks).*

- The use of the left and right buttons can be swapped (for you lefties out there).

- A trail of mouse pointers that follow the pointer movement can be turned on or off. This will drive an unsuspecting user up the wall.

Try It, You'll Like It Always use the TEST area to try new settings before leaving the screen. For example, if you set the Double Click Speed all the way to Fast, you may not be able to double-click fast enough for it to register.

To modify these settings, follow these steps:

1. From the Control Panel, open the Mouse icon. The Mouse dialog box appears.

2. Enter the settings as desired and test them in the TEST area.

3. Select OK or press Enter to accept the changes you have made. Press Esc or select Cancel to close the dialog box without saving changes.

Changing Keyboard Settings

You can change how long it takes for a key to be repeated and how fast a key repeats when it is held down. Follow these steps to change the response of the keyboard:

1. From the Control Panel, open the Keyboard icon. The Keyboard dialog box appears.

2. Enter the settings as desired and test them out in the Test area.

3. Select OK or press Enter to accept the changes you have made. Press Esc or select Cancel to close the dialog box without saving changes.

Sound Control

Controlling sounds associated with actions or events can be simple or complex. At the simplest level, you can control the warning beep when you make an error or perform an action Windows does not recognize. If you have a sound card in your computer, you can set sounds for a variety of events in Windows.

To affect sound, follow these steps:

1. From the Control Panel, open the Sound icon. The Sound dialog box appears.

2. If you do not have a sound card in your computer, the Events and Files selections are grayed-out and unavailable. To turn off the warning beep, leave the Enable System Sounds box blank. To enable the warning beep, make sure that box is checked.

3. If you have a sound card, you can select the different Events and, for each, assign a Files sound. Use Test to test out your sound selection. Also, make sure Enable System Sounds is checked.

4. Select OK or press Enter to accept the changes you have made. Press Esc or select Cancel to close the dialog box without saving changes.

Changing Ports

If you will be communicating with another computer or installing a new printer, you may need to change the settings for the port to which the modem or printer will be connected.

Through the Port icon, you can set the **B**aud Rate, **D**ata Bits, **P**arity, **S**top Bits, and **F**low Control. Most manuals for communications software and hardware specify the settings that must be used. If you have trouble, contact the manufacturer or support line for the product(s) involved. To change port settings, follow these steps:

1. From the Control Panel, open the Ports icon.

2. Select the port designation (COM1 through COM4) assigned to the port you will use.

3. The dialog box appears containing the settings for that port.

4. Enter the settings as instructed by the manual or technical support person.

5. Select OK or press Enter to accept the changes you have made. Press Esc or select Cancel to close the dialog box without saving changes.

Creating a Document with Write

In this lesson, you will create and print a letter using the Windows Write program.

Creating a Document

You may use Windows Write to create any document. This may include letters, memos, reports, lists, newsletters, and so on.

To create a document, follow these steps:

1. From the Program Manager window, open the Accessories group icon.

2. Open the Write program-item icon.

3. The Write window (shown in Figure 22.1) appears. As soon as you begin typing, you are creating a document.

Notice these portions of the Write screen in Figure 22.1:

- Application name (Write).

Program Manager Window   Application Name   Document Name

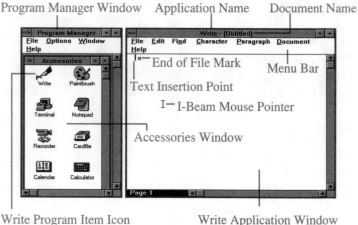

Write Program Item Icon   Write Application Window

Figure 22.1   The Windows Write window.

- Document name (Untitled for now; a name is assigned when you save the document).

- The menu bar containing the Write menus.

- Scroll bars to move through the document.

- The text insertion point which marks the spot that text you enter will be placed.

- The I-beam mouse pointer that is used to move the text insertion point. Notice that as you point at the menu bar, the pointer changes back to the arrow pointer.

Entering Text

To enter text, begin typing. Do not press Enter at the end of each line (although you can if you like). Just allow the text to wrap around. Press Enter to mark the end of a paragraph.

Figure 22.2 shows a Write screen after entering text.

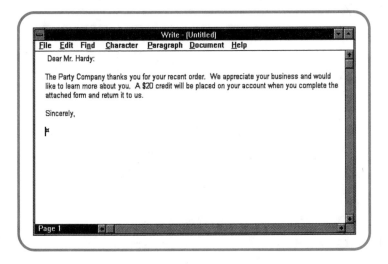

Figure 22.2 Text typed in the Write document.

Basic Editing

Everyone makes mistakes. Everyone changes his or her mind. When that happens, you can easily edit the document. Following are the specific techniques you'll use to edit your Write documents.

Moving the Text Insertion Point

To move the insertion point with the mouse, just point and click. To move the insertion point with the keyboard, see the options in Table 22.1. You can use these keys without disturbing existing text.

Table 22.1 Moving the Insertion Point with the Keyboard

Key	Movement
↓	Down a line
↑	Up a line
→	Right one character
←	Left one character
PageUp	Previous screen
PageDown	Next screen
Ctrl-→	Previous word
Ctrl-←	Next word
Ctrl-PageUp	Top of screen
Ctrl-PageDown	Bottom of screen
Home	Start of line
End	End of line
Ctrl-Home	Start of document
Ctrl-End	End of document

Inserting Text

To insert text among existing characters, simply place the insertion point (using the mouse or the keyboard) in the appropriate location and begin typing. The characters move to the right as you type.

Selecting Text

Before you edit a block of text, you first need to select it. For example, you need to select the text before you can copy it.

To use a mouse to select text:

1. Put the mouse pointer (I-beam) at the start of the text to select.

2. Press and hold down the mouse button.

3. Drag the mouse until the text selection is highlighted.

4. Release the mouse button.

Quickly Select an Entire Word   To select a word, double-click on the word. If you double-click and hold down the last click, you can extend your selection by dragging the mouse pointer.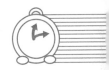

Select an Entire Paragraph   When you move the mouse pointer to the left side of the Write window, it changes into an arrow that points to the right. Click the mouse button to select the entire line or double-click to select the entire paragraph.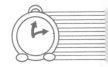

To select text with the keyboard, follow these steps:

1. Place the insertion point before the first character of the text to be selected.

2. Press and hold down the Shift key.

3. Move the insertion point to the last character in the selection.

4. Release the Shift key.

Quickly Select an Entire Word To select an entire word using the keyboard, move the insertion point to the beginning of the word. Hold down the Shift key and the Ctrl key and use the arrow keys to highlight the words you want to edit.

 Select the Entire Document Press Ctrl-Home to move the insertion point to the beginning of the document. Hold down the Shift and Ctrl keys and press the End key.

Deleting Text

To delete a single character, press the Backspace key to delete the character to the left. Press the Delete key to delete the character to the right. To delete larger amounts of text, select the text then press the Delete key.

Copying and Moving Text

You may copy or move text from one location to another.

To copy or move text, follow these steps:

1. Select the text to copy or cut.

2. Choose Edit, Copy, or Cut from the menu bar.

3. Place your insertion point where you want to paste the text.

4. Choose Edit, Paste.

Basic Formatting

You can affect the appearance of your document on-screen and when printed by changing the formatting. Formatting refers to the appearance of a document, including character style and font, line spacing, and page layout.

Character Style

Write has five basic character styles (Bold, Italic, Underline, Superscript, and Subscript). To select (or deselect) the style of characters:

1. Select the Character menu, and then select the desired style. (The style will be used if a check mark appears before it. To cancel all styles, select Regular.)

2. Type your text. The text appears in the styles with the check mark.

Changing Existing Text If you have already entered text and wish to change the character style, select the text and then set the character style.

You can also change the fonts that are used in your document. Select Character, Fonts... to access the Fonts dialog box, shown in Figure 22.3. You can choose a font before you enter the text, or you can select text you've entered and change the font.

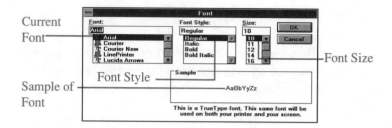

Figure 22.3 The Font dialog box.

Adjusting Margins

You may change the size of the margins from the default 1" top and bottom margin and 1.25" right and left margin. To change margins, follow these steps:

1. Select **D**ocument, **P**age Layout.

2. Type the margins you wish to use.

3. Select OK.

Line Spacing

Line spacing refers to the amount of space between lines. Follow these steps to change line spacing:

1. Put the insertion point in the paragraph to change.

2. Choose **P**aragraph, **S**ingle Space, **1** 1/2 Space, or **D**ouble Space.

3. The line spacing for the paragraph changes.

Save the Write Document

Whether you are creating a Write document or another type of document file, *always* save your work often.

Better Saved Than Sorry   When in doubt, save your document. It is better to save often than to risk losing hours of effort.

To save a Write document, follow these steps:

1. Choose File, Save.

2. If the document *has not* been saved before, the Save As dialog box shown in Figure 22.4 appears. Select the directory you want to save the document in and enter the name you want to assign to the document. Select OK.

   If the document *has* been saved before, Write will simply save the changes you made.

3. Once the document is saved, you are returned to the document window to continue work or to exit.

Notice that in Figure 22.4, the WRITEDOC directory is selected (the file folder symbol appears open and the files in the directory appear on the left). When OK is selected, the file LET1 will be saved to the WRITEDOC directory.

What About the File Extension?   Write automatically assigns the .WRI extension to files created in Write. Notice that the file name is displayed in the title bar.

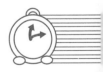

New File Name   Directory List Box

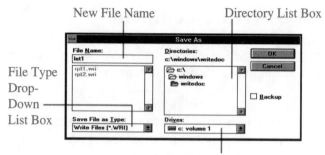

File Type
Drop-
Down
List Box

Drive Selection Drop-Down List Box

Figure 22.4   The dialog box for saving a new document.

Print the Document

Once your document is complete, you can print it. Follow these steps:

1. Choose File, Print.

2. The Print dialog box appears.

3. Identify the number of copies (if more than one) and the pages to print (if applicable) and select OK.

4. A dialog box appears to let you know the document is printing. To cancel the print job, press Cancel.

When What You See Is Not What You Get
Sometimes the document doesn't print as planned. If there are formatting or document appearance problems, your problem is within the Write document.

Lesson 23

Adding Graphics with Paintbrush

In this lesson, you will learn how to add graphics using Windows Paintbrush.

Opening Paintbrush

Paintbrush allows you to give your documents an artistic touch. To open a Paintbrush document, follow these steps:

1. From the Program Manager, open the Accessories group icon.

2. Open the Paintbrush program-item icon (see Figure 23.1).

3. The Paintbrush screen shown in Figure 23.1 appears.

In addition to familiar parts, the Paintbrush window shown in Figure 23.1 has a set of drawing tools (called the *toolbox*) on the left along with a *color palette* on the bottom of the window.

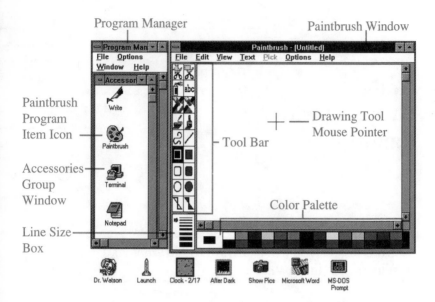

Figure 23.1 The Paintbrush screen.

Background and Foreground Colors The box within a box to the left of the color palette shows the currently selected *foreground* and *background* colors. The foreground color is the color you'll use when you draw and the background color is the color of the backdrop.

The *linesize box* on the lower left of the window identifies the width of a line when you draw. Figure 23.2 shows each of the tools in the toolbox.

Scissors		Pick
Airbrush		Text Tool
Color Brush		Eraser
Paint Roller		Brush
Curve		Line Tool
Box		Filled Box
Rounded Box		Filled Rounded Box
Circle/Ellipse		Filled Circle/Ellipse
Polygon		Filled Polygon

Figure 23.2   The tools in the toolbox.

Drawing

While you can use the keyboard to draw objects, you will find the mouse much easier. These are the steps you'll follow to draw:

1. To select the background color, point at a color in the palette and click the right mouse button.

2. To select the foreground color, point at the color in the palette and click the left mouse button.

3. To select the size of your drawing, choose Options, Image Attributes, and enter the Width and Height in the Image Attributes dialog box (see Figure 23.3).

4. Choose File, New to open a new document with the settings you entered in steps 1–3.

5. Select a drawing tool from the toolbox at the left of the screen.

6. To select the line width, click on the linesize in the box in the lower left of the screen.

7. To draw an object, point at the area where you want the object to appear and drag the mouse pointer until the object is the size you desire.

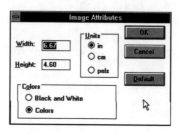

Figure 23.3   The Image Attributes dialog box.

Oops!   If you add to your graphic and decide you don't like the addition, choose Edit, Undo (or press Alt-Backspace) to undo the change you made. Use this option carefully, all changes you have made since you last changed tools will be undone.

A Perfect Circle Every Time   To draw a perfect circle, hold down the Shift key as you drag the mouse pointer. This technique can also be used to help you draw a perfect square and a perfectly straight line.

Adding Text

To add text to a graphic, follow these steps:

1. Select the Text tool.

2. Choose Text, Font.

3. From the Font dialog box, select the Font, Font Style, and Size and select OK.

4. Place the insertion point where you want to begin entering text.

5. Type the text.

Once You Leave, You Can Never Get Back   You can't edit text once you have accepted it; you can only erase it. Because of this, be sure that what you've typed is correct before you move on.

Figure 23.4 displays a graphic with text created in Paintbrush. The selected Font is Arial (supplied by Windows). The Font Style is Bold. The Size is 20. As you can see, Paintbrush can create a company letterhead, cards, diagrams, charts, or any other graphic need.

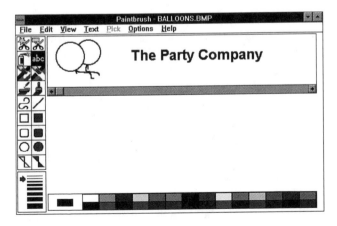

Figure 23.4   The balloon graphic with added text.

Using The Keyboard

You can use the keyboard to draw (but you probably won't like it). The keys shown in Table 23.1 may be substituted for the mouse activities.

Table 23.1 Keys Used to Draw

Key	Mouse Operation
Insert	Press left mouse button
F9-Insert	Double-click on left mouse button
Delete	Press right mouse button
F9-Delete	Double-click right mouse button
Insert-*Arrow keys*	Drag the mouse to draw

Saving the Drawing

Paintbrush allows you to save your work in a number of different formats. These include several bitmap formats (varying number of colors) and PCX, a common PC graphic file format. What format you choose depends on what you want to do with the file. If you plan to import the file into another program, make sure that you choose a format that the program can import. To save the drawing, follow these steps:

1. Choose File, Save.

2. If the file has not been saved before, choose a directory to save it in, name it, and select OK.

Printing the Drawing

To print the drawing:

1. Choose File, Print.

2. Complete the Print dialog box.

3. Select OK.

Lesson 24

Managing Time with the Accessories

In this lesson, you will learn how to use Windows' Calendar and Clock to manage your time more efficiently.

The Calendar

Windows' Calendar is handy to keep track of your daily or monthly schedule. Maintaining appointments, birthdays, holidays, and deadlines with the Calendar can help organize your life. And, if you tend to get engrossed with your work at the computer and forget the time, you can set an alarm to tell you when to quit.

Using the Calendar

To use the Calendar, follow these steps:

1. From the Program Manager, open the Accessories group icon.

2. Open the Calendar icon. A screen like the one shown in Figure 24.1 appears.

3. Choose View, Month, or Day to view the current month or current day display. Figure 24.1 displays the Day View, Figure 24.2 displays the Month View.

4. To view a day from a month calendar view, select the day and press Enter.

5. From a day calendar, you may view or edit the information for the day. You may also set an alarm for the time line where your insertion point rests. Choose Alarm, Set to set an alarm for a particular time.

6. Select Show, and then select Today, Previous, Next, or Date... to change days.

7. When you are done using the Calendar, choose File, Save, enter a file name, and choose OK.

8. To leave the Calendar, choose File, Exit.

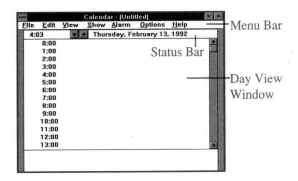

Figure 24.1 The Calendar screen—the Day View.

Table 24.1 lists shortcut keys you can use to move around in the Calendar.

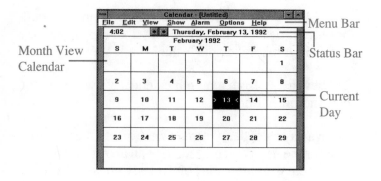

Month View
Calendar ── Menu Bar

Status Bar

Current
Day

Figure 24.2 The Calendar screen—the Month View.

Table 24.1 Calendar's Shortcut Keys

Shortcut Key Sequence	Description
F8	Displays day view
F9	Displays month view
Ctrl-PageDown	Display next month/day
Ctrl-PageUp	Displays previous month/day
F5	Set alarm on day and time

Double-click in the status bar of the calendar (with the date) to switch between Day and Month View.

Printing the Calendar

To print your appointments, follow these steps:

1. From the Calendar, choose File, Print.

2. The Print dialog box, shown in Figur‹

3. Enter the date to print **From** and **To**.

4. Select OK.

Figure 24.3 The Calendar's Print dialog box.

Handling the Clock

Windows' Clock can keep you on time. It may be displayed as an analog clock (see Figure 24.4) or a digital clock (see Figure 24.5).

Figure 24.4 The analog clock.

To use the Clock, follow these steps:

1. From the Program Manager, open the Accessories group icon.

2. Open the Clock icon.

3. To switch between analog and digital display, choose Settings, Analog, or Digital.

4. Close the clock using the Control menu.

Figure 24.5   The digital clock.

Time on My Hands, and My Windows   The Clock has a nice feature that allows you to keep it in view at all times. First minimize the Clock. It still keeps time, even as an icon. Next, move it to a position where it will not be in the way and you will be able to see it. Finally, open the Control menu and choose Always on Top. When this option is active, a check mark appears next to it on the menu. This will keep the icon on top of all other windows, where you can always see it.

In this lesson, you learned how to manage time with the Calendar and Clock.

Index

What's New in Windows 3.1

Enhancements to SETUP

Setting up your Windows environment is made easy with **Express Setup**. All you have to do is enter your name and answer a few easy questions such as where you want Windows installed and what printer you have. If you need more control over the installation process, you can still choose **Custom Setup**. *(See the Inside Front Cover.)*

Online Tutorial

Windows 3.1 comes with an **online tutorial** in which you can practice most of the skills you'll need to operate in the Windows environment.

Online Help Enhancements

Windows' online Help facility has been upgraded to include **context-sensitive help**. This means that what you see when you enter the Help program depends on what you were doing when you started Help. This is available for most of the applications that come with Windows.

Startup Configuration

Windows 3.1 provides a group named **Startup** in the Program Manager. By placing a program-item icon in this group, the application is automatically started when you enter Windows.

Customize Your Desktop

Windows now comes with more predefined **color schemes** (including 3 for use with LCD monitors) and **wallpapers** for you to make your desktop your own. **Screen savers** (with password protection) have also been added. *(See Lesson 20.)*